Langford Lovell Price

A Short History of Political Economy in England

From Adam Smith to Arnold Toynbee

Langford Lovell Price

A Short History of Political Economy in England
From Adam Smith to Arnold Toynbee

ISBN/EAN: 9783744645010

Printed in Europe, USA, Canada, Australia, Japan

Cover: Foto ©Suzi / pixelio.de

More available books at **www.hansebooks.com**

UNIVERSITY EXTENSION SERIES

EDITED BY J. E. SYMES, M.A.,
Principal of University College, Nottingham

POLITICAL ECONOMY
IN ENGLAND

University Extension Series.

UNDER the above title MESSRS. METHUEN are publishing a series of books on historical, literary, and economic subjects, suitable for extension students and home-reading circles. The volumes are intended to assist the lecturer, and not to usurp his place. Each volume will be complete in itself, and the subjects will be treated by competent writers in a broad and philosophic spirit.

THE INDUSTRIAL HISTORY OF ENGLAND. By H. DE B. GIBBINS, M.A. *[Ready.*

" A compact and clear story of our industrial development. A study of his concise but luminous book cannot fail to give the reader a clear insight into the principal phenomena of our industrial history. The editor and publishers are to be congratulated on this first volume of their venture, and we shall look with expectant interest for the succeeding volumes of the series. If they maintain the same standard of excellence the series will make a permanent place for itself among the many series which appear from time to time."—*University Extension Journal.*

PROBLEMS OF POVERTY: An Inquiry into the Industrial Conditions of the Poor. By J. A. HOBSON, M.A. *[March.*

THE FRENCH REVOLUTION. By J. E. SYMES, M.A. *[In the Press.*

VICTORIAN POETS. By A. SHARP. *[April.*

THE EVOLUTION OF PLANT LIFE: Lower Forms. By G. MASSEE. *[In the Press.*

ENGLISH SOCIAL REFORMERS. By H. DE B. GIBBINS, M.A.

NAPOLEON. By E. L. S. HORSBURGH, M.A.

ENGLISH POLITICAL HISTORY. By T. J. LAWRENCE, M.A.

SHAKESPEARE. By F. H. TRENCH, M.A.

THE ENGLISH LANGUAGE. By G. C. MOORE-SMITH, M.A.

AN INTRODUCTION TO PHILOSOPHY. By J. SOLOMON, M.A.

PSYCHOLOGY. By F. S. GRANGER, M.A. *[In the Press.*

ENGLISH PAINTERS. By D. S. MACCOLL, M.A.

ENGLISH ARCHITECTURE. By ERNEST RADFORD, M.A.

THE CHEMISTRY OF LIFE AND HEALTH. By C. W. KIMMINS, M.A.

A SHORT HISTORY

OF

POLITICAL ECONOMY IN ENGLAND

FROM ADAM SMITH TO ARNOLD TOYNBEE

BY

L. L. PRICE, M.A.,

Fellow of Oriel College, Oxford
AUTHOR OF "INDUSTRIAL PEACE"

𝕷𝖔𝖓𝖉𝖔𝖓

METHUEN AND CO., 18, BURY STREET, W.C.

1891

RICHARD CLAY & SONS, LIMITED,
LONDON & BUNGAY.

PREFACE.

IN the following pages an attempt is made to give a short account of the History of Political Economy in England from Adam Smith to Arnold Toynbee. The history is not carried back beyond Adam Smith for a reason which is stated in the chapter upon that author, and it ends with Arnold Toynbee, because the work of writers who are still living is, it may be hoped, not yet fully completed. The death of one of the best known of those writers, Professor Thorold Rogers, whose work was so original and comprehensive in conception, and so industriously and exhaustively executed, that it is to be feared that even the labours of the greater part of a life-time have failed to complete it, occurred during the time when the history was being written.

The method which has been pursued by the writer has been, while endeavouring to mention every author of importance, to select for especial consideration in separate chapters those economists, whose writings have marked distinct and recognised stages in the development of economic knowledge ; and, while noticing the main incidents of their lives, the circumstances under which their opinions were formed and expressed, and the character of their economic work generally, to concentrate special attention on that part which is either most usually associated with their

names, or seems to be the most characteristic and important.
The accounts of these special contributions to the advancement of economic inquiry are, as far as possible, given in
the language of the authors themselves; and they are
generally followed by some estimate of their relations to
more recent economic thought.

In this critical estimate an attempt is made to express the
general drift of subsequent opinion rather than the particular
views of the writer of this history, which does not put forward
any pretensions to originality. The author has freely used
all the sources of information and instruction which he has
been able to discover; and, although he has embraced every
opportunity, which seemed naturally to present itself without
burdening the notes, of acknowledging his special indebtedness to particular authorities on certain points, he is under
a general obligation which can only be fittingly discharged in
a preface. He is indebted to all who have in any way, by
commentary on the great writers of the past, or independent
development of their theories, helped to elucidate the history
of a branch of knowledge of which England may perhaps
claim to be the classic home, although she has often, and
more especially of recent times, experienced the benefits of
suggestion and criticism at the hands of foreign writers.

To Professor Symes, the editor of this series, the author
desires to express his thanks for suggestions regarding the
general plan of the book.

Oriel College, Oxford,
   8th December, 1890.

CONTENTS.

CONTENTS.

CHAPTER II.

THOMAS ROBERT MALTHUS. (1766—1834.)

THE PRINCIPLE OF POPULATION.

CHAPTER III.

DAVID RICARDO. (1772—1823.)

THE THEORY OF RENT.

CHAPTER VI.

WALTER BAGEHOT. (1826—1877.)

THE MONEY MARKET.

CHAPTER VII.

WILLIAM STANLEY JEVONS. (1835—1882.)

STATISTICS.

CHAPTER VIII.

HENRY FAWCETT. (1833—1884.)
ARNOLD TOYNBEE. (1852—1883.)

SOCIAL REFORM.

A SHORT HISTORY

OF

POLITICAL ECONOMY IN ENGLAND.

CHAPTER I.

ADAM SMITH. 1723—1790.

THE DIVISION OF LABOUR.

The Influence of the *Wealth of Nations*—Adam Smith's Life—The State of English Agriculture, and Manufactures, and Foreign Trade —Adam Smith's Passion for 'Natural Liberty'—His Relation to the Physiocrats—His Moral Philosophy—His Idea of a " Scotchman inside every Man "—Qualifications of 'Natural Liberty'—His Memory and Fertility of Illustration—Summary of the *Wealth of Nations*—Maxims of Taxation—Adam Smith's Treatment of the *Division of Labour*—Its various Forms—Its Advantages: (1) Increase of Skill—(2) Saving of Skill—Possible Disadvantages—(3) Introduction of Machinery—(4) Saving of Time—Its implied Conditions— The Mechanism of Exchange—The Origin and Use of Money—Its Functions as (1) a Medium of Exchange—(2) A Measure of Value— The True Nature of the Work performed by it—Adam Smith's Vindication of Free Trade resting on (1) Division of Labour between Nations—(2) The Nature of Money—The Mercantile System— Application to present Controversies.

THE first great name in the history of English Political Economy is that of ADAM SMITH. It is true that much of the argument presented in his *Wealth of Nations* may be traced in faint and broken outline on the pages of previous

B

writers,[1] just as it is true that it would be an egregious mistake to suppose that he pronounced the last word on many of the topics of which he treated. But his work furnishes the most convenient and appropriate starting-point for investigation, backwards or forwards. If we examine closely the thought of those economists who preceded him, we find that he has presented it in such a form, that in his hands it may be regarded as new ; and, if we look carefully into the writings of those who have come after him, we discover that in many cases he may without unfairness be described as having anticipated the essential points of their teaching. If, then, a classification were made of those authors whose writings had constituted epochs in the history of economic science, the chief place would be given by almost universal consent to Adam Smith ; and, if any economic book could be styled immortal, the *Wealth of Nations* would be the first to earn that title.

Within fifteen years of its publication Adam Smith died ; but it had already passed into six editions, and had been translated into the chief European languages. It had been read with such appreciation by Pitt that Adam Smith had declared that the statesman understood the book as well as himself; and a competent observer of the current of opinion had ventured on the prediction that the author would " persuade the living generation, and govern the next." Nor has this prophecy been shown by the subsequent course of events to be without foundation, although the exact date of its fulfilment may have been postponed for a generation or two. The book has exercised an influence in practical affairs which might have filled Adam Smith with astonishment. He remarked that to "expect" "that the freedom of trade"

[1] Such as Sir Dudley North in his *Discourses upon Trade* (1691).

—for which he so earnestly contended—"should ever be entirely restored in Great Britain," was " as absurd as to expect that an Oceana or Utopia should ever be established in it." And yet, largely through the influence, direct or indirect, of his teaching, that "freedom of trade" has been "entirely restored." The language of an economist of our own times, who was also a practical man of the world, is by no means that of mere idle exaggeration. He says[1] that the *Wealth of Nations* has had a "wonderful effect." "The life of almost every one in England—perhaps of every one—is different and better in consequence of it." "No other form of political philosophy has ever had one thousandth part of the influence on us; its teachings have settled down into the common sense of the nation, and have become irreversible."

What, then, has been the secret of this unique and almost magical influence? We may perhaps find some answer to our question in the circumstances surrounding the life of Adam Smith. At first sight it might indeed seem as if that life were uneventful. He was born at Kirkcaldy, in Fifeshire, in 1723, and was brought up by his mother, who had lost her husband—a comptroller of Customs—before his birth. He was educated, first at the grammar-school of his native town, and then at the University of Glasgow, where he studied mathematics and natural philosophy, and from whence he proceeded, as Snell Exhibitioner, to Balliol College, Oxford. Here he continued to reside for seven years, devoting himself especially to the study of moral and political science, and serving his term of 'apprenticeship' to the mastership of arts; and then he returned to Kirkcaldy, and, after some two years had passed, began to

[1] Bagehot, *Economic Studies*, p. 1.

lecture on rhetoric and *belles-lettres* in Edinburgh.   He
formed an enduring friendship with the philosopher, David
Hume,[1] and won such a reputation that, in 1751, he was
appointed Professor of Logic, and, in the succeeding year,
Professor of Moral Philosophy, in the University of Glasgow.
The substance of part of the lectures he delivered from the
latter chair was afterwards embodied in the *Wealth of
Nations;* and he himself describes his tenure of the pro-
fessorship as "by far the most useful, and therefore by far
the happiest and most honourable period of" his "life."   In
1759 he published a treatise on the *Theory of Moral
Sentiments,* and in 1763 he received an invitation to
accompany the young Duke of Buccleuch on his foreign
travels.   He accepted the invitation and resigned his pro-
fessorship; and he remained abroad until 1766, when he
returned to Kirkcaldy, and devoted himself to the composition of his great work.   This was published in 1776, and
he spent most of the two following years in London, in the
enjoyment of the best society.   In 1778 he was appointed
a Commissioner of Customs for Scotland, and took up his
residence in Edinburgh.   In 1787 he was elected Lord
Rector of his old University of Glasgow, and in 1790 he
died at the age of sixty-seven.

Such a life as this might at first sight seem to be but a
tranquil and uneventful career; and yet it is not difficult to
gather from it many hints of the influences which moulded
the character of his writing, and contributed to secure for
it such remarkable success.

In the first place he lived at the close of an old industrial

---

[1] Hume devoted some essays to the treatment of economic subjects,
such as Interest, Money and the Balance of Trade, and may have influenced Adam Smith in no inconsiderable degree.

era, and before the full commencement of a new. He lived
at a time when the rules and regulations, by which in very
many cases the prosecution of industry was directed, had
lost the reason they had formerly possessed in the circumstances of the times, and were becoming the useless and
vexatious relics of a by-gone age. During the greater part
of his life the agricultural industry of the country was still
carried on in many places under nearly the same system as
that which had prevailed in the Middle Ages. In many
places there were still open, unenclosed fields, with holdings
made up of small scattered parcels, and common rights of
pasture over the stubble of the arable and the grass of the
meadow land. "A very great part of the country," writes
Adam Smith himself, "still remains uncultivated;" and the
general system of cultivation was of a wretched description.
There was no proper order of rotation of crops, no scientific
breeding of cattle, no turnips or artificial grasses, except
in particular districts like Norfolk, where Townshend was
already earning the complimentary nickname of 'Turnip
Townshend,' and Leicestershire, where Bakewell was beginning to attract visitors from all parts of the world to learn
the true principles of the grazier's art. But these modern
improvements were confined for the most part to the counties
where they originated; and throughout the rest of the country
the primitive unscientific methods still prevailed, while
quarrels were often arising on questions of boundaries and
rights of pasture.

Nor was the state of affairs different in manufacturing
industry; for here too there were vexatious regulations and
coercive routine. The very word 'manufacturer' had not
yet lost its original meaning of one who worked with his
hands, for industrial occupations were pursued for the most

part under what is known as the 'domestic system' by craftsmen working with their own hands in their own houses. There were, indeed, even at this time some instances of capitalist employers, or, as Adam Smith calls them, 'undertakers,' after the modern pattern; but he almost invariably uses the term 'manufacturer' in its original sense. In many cases a workman was unable to practise a handicraft unless he had served a regular apprenticeship, and received the license of a trade-corporation. The number of apprentices a craftsman could have was, together with the term of their service, regulated in many towns and trades expressly by statute, and in others by custom which was as binding as law; and a workman, who moved from one district to another, exposed himself to the risk of being sent back to his original parish, under the provisions of the Law of Settlement, for fear that he might eventually come upon the rates in his new abode. The woollen industry was now, as it had for some time been, the staple industry of the country; but Adam Smith observes[1] that only three mechanical inventions of importance had been introduced since the reign of Edward IV. The iron industry, which was largely carried on in Sussex, where it was still possible to see the iron smelted by charcoal in small furnaces blown by leathern bellows worked by oxen, was dying out; and the cotton industry was so insignificant as to be mentioned only once, and then incidentally, in the *Wealth of Nations*.

Apart, however, from the serious restrictions imposed on labour by the 'exclusive' trade-corporations, the 'ill-contrived' law of settlement, and the statute and custom of apprenticeship, the 'inland trade' of the country was, in

[1] Toynbee (*Industrial Revolution*, p. 51) says that he "forgot to mention" a fourth.

Adam Smith's words, " almost perfectly free," although the
want of adequate means of communication formed a
serious hindrance to its development.   But, in contrast with
the 'inland trade,' the external commerce was hampered
by a number of vexatious restrictions.   It was regulated
with a view to securing what was known as a 'favourable
balance' of trade, by making, if possible, the exports greater
than the imports, and by endeavouring to procure the
amount due for this excess in actual bullion. " High duties,"
and in some instances "absolute prohibitions," were employed
as "restraints upon the importation of foreign goods," and
" exportation was encouraged, sometimes by drawbacks,
sometimes by bounties, sometimes by advantageous treaties
of commerce with foreign states, and sometimes by the
establishment of colonies in distant countries."   For these
colonies were regarded as a field for the commercial
'monopoly' of the mother-country, and of the chartered
companies to which in some instances their government had
been intrusted.

On all sides, then; there were regulations and restrictions,
when the season for restriction and regulation, which had
once existed, was passing away.   There is perhaps no more
suggestive illustration of this than the story told of James
Watt, the inventor of the steam-engine, who betook himself
to Glasgow, and, after the local corporation of 'hammer-
men' had refused to give him permission to practise his
trade, was admitted within the walls of the University, and
allowed to set up his workshop.

The consideration, which was specially impressed upon
Adam Smith's mind by these circumstances, was the paramount need of freedom.   It has been said [1]—not perhaps

---

[1] Toynbee, *Industrial Revolution*, p. 14.

without exaggeration—that this was the "first and the last word of his political and industrial philosophy"; and it is true that "every page of" his "writings is illumined" by the "passion for freedom." "Break down," he exclaims, "the exclusive privilege of corporations, and repeal the statute of apprenticeship, both which are real encroachments upon natural liberty, and add to these the repeal of the law of settlement."

But what does he mean by 'natural liberty'? Here we come upon another of the great moulding influences of his life. His 'passion for freedom' was not merely the practical outcome of a reaction against restrictive routine, but it had also a basis in theoretical speculation. He had, as we have seen, accepted at one period of his life what we may perhaps call a 'travelling tutorship,' and a considerable part of the time he spent abroad had been passed in Paris. At that date there was a group of philosophers and reformers in France, "a few men," as Adam Smith called them, "of great learning and ingenuity," who are known by the name of the Physiocrats, or adherents of the rule of nature. They, like him, were impatient with the vexatious regulations which hampered trade, to a greater extent in their own country than in England, and like him they felt an ardent sympathy for the common people, who were robbed of the "free disposal" of their "most sacred and inviolable" property, the labour of their hands, by these restrictions. They held that, if they could once remove this overgrowth of artificial regulation, they would find beneath it the simplicity of nature. They believed in the current philosophy, which maintained that there had once been a state of nature, and that, when society was established, men had entered into an engagement—a 'social contract,' as it was sometimes called—

to surrender some of the individual rights they then enjoyed, which might conflict with the rights of their fellow-men. And they argued that existing human institutions should be made to conform, as far as was possible, to the original simplicity of nature, when all men were equal and free. This was what was meant by 'natural liberty.' "All systems," writes Adam Smith, who in this was their disciple, X although he was careful to point out the "capital error" of their "system" of political economy, which represented agriculture "as the sole source of the revenue and wealth of every country,"—"all systems, either of preference or of restraint, therefore, being thus completely taken away, the obvious and simple system of natural liberty establishes itself of its own accord." It is scarcely an unmeaning co-incidence that the same year which saw the publication of the *Wealth of Nations* witnessed the Declaration of American Independence, in which it was formally affirmed that all men were 'by nature equal and free.'

The belief, which was thus felt by Adam Smith in the supreme value and need of 'natural liberty,' was strengthened by his moral and religious opinions. It is as impossible with him, as it is with any man, to separate entirely one part of his nature from another ; and his 'passion for freedom' was undoubtedly strengthened by the conviction, to which he gave emphatic expression in his moral treatise, that the benevolent government of the world by God would, in most cases, lead the individual, who was freely seeking his own interests, to advance the interests of the common weal. He would be "led by an invisible hand to promote an end which was no part of his intention."

Again he was a Scotchman, and he may be said to have possessed a full measure of a Scotchman's hard-headedness.

He could see through the specious and fallacious arguments
which were frequently employed in support of the restrictive
regulations of the times.   And the national characteristics
betrayed themselves in other ways; for it has been said
with considerable truth that he "seemed to think that there
was a Scotchman inside every man."   If, indeed, every one
who took part in industry possessed a Scotchman's canny
acuteness and pertinacity, if they were all as fully and
constantly alive to their interests, and as determined to seek
them, as the proverbial Scotchman is, then we might with
more complacency leave them to fight out a struggle for
industrial existence in perfect freedom.   Competition might
be entirely free, for the competitors would be equal in power
and intelligence.   But it is because individuals sometimes
allow the consideration of their immediate interests, or the
passing influence of passion, to blind them to their true
permanent interests, and it is because there are men, and
at any rate there are women and children, engaged in
industry, who start with a disadvantage, which no purely
economic forces seem likely to remove, in strength of body
or mind, or pecuniary resources—it is for these reasons that
later experience has tended to enforce the conclusion that
competition cannot, consistently with due regard to the real
and lasting prosperity of a whole nation, be entirely un-
restricted and free.   It is precisely because there is not
a "Scotchman inside every man" that 'natural liberty'
has been regulated in practice by Factory Legislation, by
Co-operation, and by Trades Unions.

But these considerations do not destroy the value of
Adam Smith's work.   Like his predecessors, the Physiocrats,
he recognised exceptions to the rule of 'natural liberty,'
though, like them, he did not lay much stress on those ex-

ceptions. The very phrase in which the principles of 'natural liberty' have since been so often summed up, "*Laissez faire, laissez aller* (or *passer*)," seems to have had originally a different meaning from that which was afterwards given to it. It meant that every one should be permitted to engage in what occupation he pleased, and to produce his wares according to the fashion he himself selected, and not that which a government dictated; and it also meant that individuals and their wares should be allowed to pass through the length and breadth of a country without being subject to tolls and restrictions. It meant, in a wider interpretation, "let everything alone which is injurious neither to good morals, nor to liberty, nor to property, nor to personal security."

And so Adam Smith will not leave education or banking entirely to the play of individual liberty, but will call in the regulating authority of the State. "Those exertions," he expressly says, when dealing with the subject of banking, "of the natural liberty of a few individuals, which might endanger the security of the whole society are, and ought to be, restrained by the laws of all governments, of the most free, as well as of the most despotical." And his condemnation of the Mercantile System, and of the disadvantages it endeavoured to impose upon foreign as contrasted with home industry, is qualified by his exception of the Act of Navigation as a measure of national defence, which "is of much more importance than opulence," and by his recognition that in some cases, where industries have been encouraged by prohibitions on foreign goods to employ a "multitude of hands," "humanity" may "require that the freedom of trade should be restored only by slow gradations, and with a good deal of reserve and circumspection."

And, again, when he says that, if the " wealth of a country " " has been long stationary," the " hands " would " naturally multiply beyond their employment," it would be a gratuitous misrepresentation of his meaning to suppose that in this passage he understands by ' naturally' anything more than what would happen if there were no interference with individual liberty, and not necessarily what should, or ought to, happen. The sense in which he uses the terms ' natural ' and ' naturally' is, it is true, fluctuating, and it is not free from confusing ambiguity; and his own confident belief in the beneficent government of the world by Divine Providence led him to think that, in the long run, and for the most part, that which would as a matter of fact result from the free action of the individual would be also that which ought to take place consistently with moral requirements.

More recent economists have substituted the expression ' normal ' for ' natural,' to avoid the associations of this particular ethical doctrine, and to emphasise the conception of economics as a science, which Adam Smith himself did not clearly distinguish from the idea of it as an art. It is only after we have gone through the difficult scientific task of working out the consequences of free competition between competitors, who are continually alive to their true permanent interests, that we can discover where that competition should in practice be modified, when we deal with the world of actual life, with all its inequalities, and ignorance, and poverty. The science of economics, like other sciences, investigates the relations between cause and effect, and states what is the case ; and the art of philanthropy or statesmanship discovers how the knowledge furnished by science should be used as a guide in practice. It has

indeed been said [1] that the chief work of Adam Smith himself was, not his forcible advocacy of the practical doctrine
of Free Trade, but his "careful and scientific inquiry into
the manner in which value measures human motive."

Later economists have thus brought into prominence
the distinction between a science and an art, which only
existed, if it existed at all, in Adam Smith's time, in a
latent form, and they have tended to make that clear which
in his writing is liable to produce confusion in the mind of
the reader, though it may not have originated in that of the
writer. But most of them would allow that it is only in
exceptional cases, to be justified on their individual merits,
that competition should be regulated, and 'natural liberty'
restricted, and they would recognise the practical wisdom
of Adam Smith's observation, that "what is the species of
domestic industry which his capital can employ, and of
which the produce is likely to be of the greatest value,
every individual, it is evident, can, in his local situation,
judge much better than any statesman or law-giver can do
for him." Nor would they be inclined to deny that the
crying need of the age in which he lived was the removal
of artificial obstruction.

For the persuasive enforcement of this he had peculiar
qualifications. He was distinguished in boyhood by a
remarkable memory, and his Glasgow lectures were rendered
attractive by his fertility of illustration. We are told that he
would often begin these lectures with some hesitation, as
though he were not quite master of his subject, but that as
he went on "the matter seemed to crowd upon him," and,
"by the fulness and variety of his illustrations, the subject
gradually swelled in his hands." He had, too, the great

[1] Marshall's *Principles of Economics*, p. 57.

advantage of the instruction derived from foreign travel, and
he had seen with his own eyes the state of affairs in France.
He had, no doubt, frequently conversed with the Glasgow
merchants, many of whom, then as now, must have been
shrewd practical men of the world; and he was able to
verify his theories by appeals to fact. From his boyhood
he had felt a passion for books which resulted, we are told,
in a library of some five thousand volumes; and on this
abundant material his excellent memory enabled him to
draw with such facility that we rarely find a note or reference
on the numerous pages of the *Wealth of Nations*. It is
this copiousness of felicitous illustration—a copiousness
which is perhaps best shown in such a chapter as that[1] on
the causes of differences of wages and profits in different
employments, and it is his wide acquaintance with actual
fact, and his constant reference to it, which have given his
work so much of its attractive and enduring interest for
practical men, and have made theoretical writers dispute
whether he constructed his theories from his facts, or used
his facts to illustrate and verify his theories.

The *Inquiry into the Nature and Causes of the Wealth of
Nations* consists of a brief Introduction, in which the "plan
of the work" is explained, and five Books. Of these the
first two deal mainly with those branches of the subject
which would now be especially comprehended under the term
'economic theory.' In the former the "causes" of "improvement" in the "productive powers of labour," and the "order
according to which its produce is naturally distributed among
the different ranks and conditions of men," form "the
subject" of inquiry; and in the latter Adam Smith examines
the "nature of capital stock" and the "manner in which it is

---

[1] Bk. I., chap. x.

gradually accumulated," and "employed" in putting "different
quantities of labour" "into motion." Translated into the
economic terminology of the present day, the contents of
these two books form Adam Smith's theory of the production
and distribution of wealth. The third is historical, and traces
the "different progress of opulence in different nations."
The "policy of some nations has," he observes, "given extraordinary encouragement to the industry of the country,
that of others to the industry of towns." These different
policies, again, "have given occasion to very different theories
of political economy," and these mistaken theories he examines in his fourth book. He investigates and exposes in
detail the "mean and malignant expedients" of that Mercantile System, which "magnified the importance of that
industry which was carried on in towns," and he explains
more briefly the "capital error" of that agricultural system
of the French Physiocrats which, "with all its imperfections,"
was "perhaps the nearest approximation to the truth that"
had "yet been published upon the subject of Political
Economy." In his fifth and concluding book he treats of
the "revenue of the sovereign or commonwealth," as distinct from the "revenue of the great body of the people,"
which had been brought under consideration in all the
preceding books.

It is in the course of this book that he states and explains
those four maxims of taxation which have since been
associated with his name. The maxim of *equality* enjoins
that the "subjects of every state ought to contribute towards
the support of the government, as nearly as possible, in
proportion to their respective abilities; that is, in proportion
to the revenue which they respectively enjoy under the
protection of the state." The second maxim is that of

certainty. "The tax which each individual is bound to pay ought to be certain, and not arbitrary. The time of payment, the manner of payment, the quantity to be paid, ought all to be clear and plain to the contributor, and to every other person." According to the third maxim, which is that of *convenience,* "every tax ought to be levied at the time or in the manner in which it is most likely to be convenient for the contributor to pay it." The fourth and last maxim may be called that of *economy;* for, according to it, "every tax ought to be so contrived as both to take out and to keep out of the pockets of the people as little as possible, over and above what it brings into the public treasury of the state." These maxims have been criticised in detail by subsequent writers; but they have been generally accepted in English theory, and have been often applied to English practice.

In the opening sentences of his treatise Adam Smith traces the wealth of nations to its original source in labour. The "annual labour of every nation is," he remarks, "the fund which originally supplies it with all the necessaries and conveniences of life which it annually consumes," and the produce of this labour depends in the main "on the skill, dexterity, and judgment with which" it is "generally applied." Thus he is led to discuss in the first chapter of Book I. the "Division of Labour"; for the "greater part" of this skill, dexterity and judgment seem to "have been the effects" of its systematic application. His treatment of the subject has been recently described[1] by a critical writer as an "unrivalled exposition," and it has always occupied a prominent place in the history of economic science. We may therefore examine it with some minute-

[1] Ingram's *History of Political Economy,* p. 94.

ness as supplying a typical illustration of his method ; and we shall find that it will form a convenient introduction to some of the more important and notable parts of the rest of his work.

With that appreciation of the value of actual fact which characterises his writing throughout, he explains the nature of the division of labour " by considering in what manner it operates in some particular manufactures "; and he selects an example, which has since become 'classical,' from the " trade of the pin-maker." ' He shows how " one man draws out the wire, another straights it, a third cuts it, a fourth points it, a fifth grinds it at the top for receiving the head," how "to make the head requires two or three distinct operations," how "to put it on is a peculiar business," and "to whiten the pins is another," how "it is even a trade by itself to put them into the paper," and how "the important business of making a pin is, in this manner, divided into about eighteen distinct operations, which, in some manu-factories, are all performed by distinct hands, though in others the same man will sometimes perform two or three of them." He points out the various forms of recognition which the principle of the division of labour has found in the history of man. | The "separation of different trades and employments from one another," which is not made in a "rude state of society," but is "carried furthest in those countries which enjoy the highest degree of industry and improvement," is one method of applying the principle. Another is the division "among a great number of hands" of the labour which is "necessary to produce any one com-plete manufacture," such, for example, as that of linen or cloth, from the "growers of the flax" in the one case to the "bleachers and smoothers of the linen," and in the other from the growers of the wool to the "dyers and dressers of the cloth." In fact, he observes, "without the assistance and *co-operation* [1] of many thousands, the very meanest person in a civilised country could not be provided, even according to, what we very falsely imagine, the easy and simple manner in which he is commonly accommodated."

Later economic inquiry has not added much to Adam Smith's description. A connection and distinction have indeed been established, which he did not render explicit; and economists have used the term '*simple co-operation*' to denote what happens when several persons help each other in the same occupation, working together "at the same time, in the same place, and in the same way," as, for instance, in the felling of trees, or the rowing of boats, and '*complex co-operation*' to express what happens when several persons help each other in different occupations. It is this latter form of 'co-operation' which is more especially known as division of labour; and it has been carried to a further point in the modern system of industry than that which it had reached in Adam Smith's day. The organisation, for instance, prevailing within a single factory is more complete than it could be under a domestic system of industry. From the employer down to the errand-boy the principle of the division of labour is systematically applied. The separation, again, of trades and occupations is pushed further, and one branch of a trade is now as distinct from another as the trades themselves were in former times. These different trades, once more, tend to settle in distinct localities, and the mutual dependence of individuals, and districts, on one another, and their mutual 'assistance and co-operation,' become continually greater.

[1] The italics are my own.

But, notwithstanding these changes and developments, Adam Smith's account of the advantages of the principle remains substantially true ; and, subject to some additions, it may still be considered adequate. These advantages are three in number. | The first is the " increase of dexterity in every particular workman." "The division of labour," he observes, " by reducing every man's business to some one simple operation, and by making this operation the sole employment of his life, necessarily increases very much the dexterity of the workman." He had, he states, seen a small pin manufactory, where ten men only, and not the full number of eighteen, were employed. And yet, " very poor " though they were, and "indifferently " as they were " accommodated with the necessary machinery," they could, by applying the principle of the division of labour, make "about twelve pounds," or upwards of forty-eight thousand pins, in a day. Each of them, therefore, might be said to have made upwards of four thousand eight hundred ; but, had they " all wrought separately and independently," " they certainly could not each of them have made twenty, perhaps not one, pin in a day."

This advantage of the division of labour has been curiously confirmed by later investigation.[1] Use, it is sometimes said, is 'second nature'; and physiologists state that, when an act has to be done for the first time, the 'sensory' or feeling nerves of the eye and the hand "send up messages " to the brain, to inform it of the position of affairs. The brain sets to work, and sends down instructions by the ' efferent ' nerves of the hand. But, when the act has been repeatedly done, an automatic connection springs up between the 'sensory' and the ' efferent ' nerves, and the act is performed without the brain being consciously called into

---

[1] Cf. Marshall's *Principles of Economics*, Bk. iv. chap. ix.

operation at all. " Use is second nature," and the brain may either employ itself on other matters, or rest quiet, ready to come forth in its full vigour when the work of the day is over. In a sense it is even possible to do two things at the same time.

The division of labour, then, *increases* the skill of the workman. But it also—and this point, unnoticed by Adam Smith, was brought into prominence by CHARLES BABBAGE [1] —effects a *saving* of skill. If the whole of the operations required in the production of an article of manufacture had to be executed by a single individual, he "must possess sufficient skill to perform the most difficult, and sufficient strength to execute the most laborious, of the operations into which the work is divided." But, by applying the principle of the division of labour, each different kind of skill and strength can be continuously and exclusively employed on the highest kind of work for which it is fitted.

It is true that this exclusive devotion of a man to some special occupation may entail certain disadvantages, and Adam Smith was not careful to notice these; for they had scarcely come into prominence at the time when he wrote. The division, and subdivision, of labour may possibly render it harder for a man to obtain employment at other work, should his own fail; for he cannot turn specialised skill to general account. But, on the other hand, they may enable him to pass with greater ease from one of the many branches into which a trade is now subdivided to the kindred branches in another trade than he could in times past have gone from trade to trade. It has been stated, as a matter of fact, that, at the close of the American Civil War, a rifle factory was

[1] Babbage wrote a book, published in 1832, *On the Economy of Machinery and Manufactures.* Cf. sec. 168.

transformed into a factory for the production of sewing machines.[1]

Again it has been alleged—and Adam Smith notices this objection in another part of his book—that the division of labour renders a man's work monotonous. But he also states that if, in civilised times, an individual's occupation be monotonous, there is "an almost infinite variety in the occupations of the whole society." If, indeed, a man's work is purely muscular, monotony seems to be unquestionably a serious evil; but, if the work is comparatively light and intellectual, the evil is by no means so great. And the division of labour does undoubtedly tend to diminish the amount of work which is merely muscular, for it permits of the more advantageous substitution of machinery.

Adam Smith declares that "the invention of all those machines, by which labour is so much facilitated and abridged, seems to have been originally owing to the division of labour." The constant observation and practice of one peculiar kind of labour would, he thought, lead men to "discover easier and readier methods of attaining" their object. "In the first fire-engines, a boy was constantly employed to open and shut alternately the communication between the boiler and the cylinder, according as the piston either ascended or descended. One of those boys, who loved to play with his companions, observed that, by tying a string from the handle of the valve which opened this communication to another part of the machine, the valve would open and shut without his assistance, and leave him

---

[1] Cf. Marshall's *Economics of Industry*, I. viii. 9. Professor Marshall points out in his *Principles of Economics*, p. 319, that the use of machinery tends to increase the demand for the *general* qualities of judgment and intelligence.

at liberty to divert himself with his playfellows." From this simple device "one of the greatest improvements" in the machine resulted; and, in some such way as this, we may believe that many inventions have been effected, which, considered individually, may seem but trifling, and yet, taken together, may amount to a transformation of a machine. " Many improvements," have also, it is true, been "made by the ingenuity of the makers of the machines"; and " some," Adam Smith observes, "by that of those who are called philosophers, or men of speculation, whose trade it is not to do anything, but to observe everything." But in both these cases, as in that which was mentioned before, the result may be ascribed to the division of labour; for, in accordance with that application of the principle which is found in the separation of employments, to make machines becomes the " business of a peculiar trade," and similarly, "in the progress of society, philosophy or speculation becomes, like every other employment, the principal or sole trade and occupation of a limited class of citizens."

The introduction of improved machinery may be ascribed to the division of labour on another ground. Adam Smith enumerates as one of the advantages of the principle the " saving " of the " time which is commonly lost " "in passing from one sort of work to another." " It is," he observes, " impossible to pass very quickly from one kind of work to another, that is carried on in a different place, and with quite different tools"; and even "when the two trades can be carried on in the same work-house," the loss of time, though "no doubt much less," is " very considerable," for a "man commonly saunters a little in turning his hand from one sort of employment to another." Later writers have indeed shown that there are considerations to be urged on the other side. " A change of occupation," Mill argues, " will often afford relief," and the " habit of passing rapidly from one occupation to another may be acquired." But on the whole we may say that here, as on other points, the subsequent course of economic inquiry has tended to confirm and to amplify Adam Smith's observations.

To the saving of time, which may be lost in passing from one occupation to another, we have now to add the saving of time spent in learning a trade, when a knowledge of a single branch only, instead of the whole, is acquired. This may, indeed, seem a doubtful advantage, but there can be no doubt about that implied in the saving of time spent in spreading the knowledge of inventions and improvements, when industries are localised in particular districts. Nor can there, again, be any question that the division of labour conduces to a saving of time, which would be lost if a machine were to stand idle; and that the introduction and use of machinery are to a very large degree dependent on the extension of the principle. They are so, because it is only in the performance of uniform operations, which are frequently repeated, that machinery is advantageous, as each special machine can execute only special work. They are so, again, because the use of machinery depends, like the division of labour, on the extent of the market.[1]

The division of labour, as Adam Smith saw, implied certain conditions. It implied freedom of labour and freedom of exchange. A man must be able, without the

[1] Senior points out (*Political Economy*, p. 74), the saving which results from the fact "that the same exertions which are necessary to produce a single given result are often sufficient to produce many hundred or many thousand similar results"; and he quotes the "forwarding of letters" through the Post Office as an illustration.

vexatious hindrance of a law of settlement, of a statute or custom of apprenticeship, or of the "exclusive privileges of corporations," to engage in the work for which he was best fitted ; and he must also be able to procure from other men the goods he might require by the free exchange of the goods he had produced, if he were not to starve for want of the necessaries of life.   The further this freedom of exchange was extended, the more likely it was that there would be a sufficient demand for the goods produced by the labour of each individual to render his exclusive devotion to his special occupation both advantageous and safe.   The division of labour, therefore, was "limited by the extent of the market."   "In the lone houses and very small villages " of the Highlands of Scotland "every-farmer must," Adam Smith observes, "be butcher, baker, and brewer for his own family" ; and the history of trade shows that "it is upon the sea-coast, and along the banks of navigable rivers," which in early times afford ampler and better means of communication than are provided by land, "that industry of every kind naturally begins to subdivide and improve itself."

These considerations led him to examine the mechanism of markets, and the different methods of exchange practised in primitive and more advanced states of society.   In early times the only method was that of direct barter, or exchange of goods for goods ; but, as the division of labour extended, and men no longer consumed themselves all that they produced, or produced themselves all that they consumed, a system of direct barter must, he remarks, "frequently have been very much clogged and embarrassed in its operations."

In the first place, there was the great inconvenience of

a 'want of coincidence,' to use the technical language of recent economic manuals. "The butcher," for example, Adam Smith writes, "has more meat in his shop than he can himself consume, and the brewer and the baker would each of them be willing to purchase a part of it; but they have nothing to offer in exchange, except the different productions of their respective trades, and the butcher is already provided with all the bread and beer which he has immediate occasion for. No exchange can, in this case, be made between them. He cannot be their merchant, nor they his customers." To "avoid," therefore, the "inconveniency of such situations, every prudent man, in every period of society, after the first establishment of the division of labour, must naturally have endeavoured to manage his affairs in such a manner as to have at all times by him, besides the peculiar produce of his own industry, a certain quantity of some one commodity or other, such as he imagined few people would be likely to refuse in exchange for the produce of their industry."

"Many different commodities," he proceeds to remark, have at different times been employed for this purpose. In the "rude ages" cattle "are said to have been the common instrument of commerce," though, he adds, "they must have been a most inconvenient one." In his own days salt was said to be thus used in Abyssinia; "a species of shells in some parts of the coast of India; dried cod at Newfoundland; tobacco in Virginia; sugar in some of our West India colonies; hides or dressed leather in some other countries." But "in all countries" "men seem at last to have been determined by irresistible reasons to give the preference" to "metals." They are not only more durable than most other commodities, but they also admit more easily of division into "any number of parts;" and this, "more than any other quality, renders them fit to be the instruments of commerce" and exchange.   Different metals have been thus employed in different countries—iron in Sparta, copper among the ancient Romans, and "gold and silver among all rich and commercial nations," for the important reason that, owing to their "utility, beauty, and scarcity," they contain a great amount of value in a small bulk. Originally, however, the metals seem to have been used in the shape of "rude bars, without any stamp or coinage"; but afterwards a "public stamp" was affixed, to attest, in the first instance, the "goodness or fineness," and, in the next place, the weight, of the metal contained in the coin.

Such is a brief outline of the account given by him of the "origin and use of money," and in this way he shows how it has become "in all civilised nations the universal instrument of commerce, by the intervention of which goods of all kinds are bought and sold, or exchanged for one another." It is, to use again the technical language of economic manuals, a 'medium of exchange.'

But in these manuals we find a second function assigned to money, which is a consequence of the first, and limits a second inconvenience of the system of barter. "When barter ceases," Adam Smith writes, "and money has become the common instrument of commerce, every particular commodity is more frequently exchanged for money than for any other commodity."   And "hence it comes to pass, that the exchangeable value of every commodity is more frequently estimated by the quantity of money than by the quantity either of labour or of any other commodity which can be had in exchange for it."   Money is thus a 'measure of value' as well as a 'medium of exchange'; and its use limits the inconvenience, which is incident to a system of barter, of "determining at what rate an exchange shall be effected."

In both these important respects the employment of money greatly facilitates the exchange of commodities, and Adam Smith was careful to show this. But he was no less careful to point out the real nature of the work performed, and his fame rests in an especial degree on his exposure of the fallacies to which erroneous opinion on the subject had led. He saw that money was a very convenient "instrument of commerce," and that wealth was generally measured by it. "We say of a rich man," he remarks, "that he is worth a great deal, and of a poor man that he is worth very little money." But he did not on that account fall into what he regarded as the mischievous errors of the Mercantile System; and his powerful vindication of Free Trade may be said to be based on the one hand on the conclusions he had drawn from the consideration of the division of labour, and, on the other, on the conception he had formed of the functions of money.

The difference between a system of exchanging by means of direct barter, and by means of money, was nothing more than this. Under the first system goods were exchanged directly for goods; the second implied the "intervention of another commodity," and goods were first exchanged for money, and then money for goods. The convenience of the transaction was immensely increased; for every one would be willing to take money for goods, knowing that he could always obtain goods for money, and it was far easier for him to make the necessary calculations, when he could compare the prices of different commodities, instead of comparing on each occasion the different commodities themselves with one another. But the essence of the matter was unaltered. It was still an exchange of commodities for commodities. Many different commodities had in times past been used for the purpose which the metals now discharged, and gold and silver were themselves commodities. They varied in their " value, " they were "sometimes cheaper and sometimes dearer," " sometimes of easier, and sometimes of more difficult purchase," and they shared, in common with other commodities, a " natural tendency " to " fly from the worse to the better market."

In some respects they might even be considered inferior to other commodities. " The gold and silver money in a country," he observed in a striking image, " may be very properly compared to a highway which, while it circulates and carries to market all the grass and corn of the country, produces itself not a single pile of either." It was, he remarked, useful as a " great but expensive instrument of commerce," but, while it was thus employed, it could not be put to other uses, and it was only by parting with it that men could obtain the real means of livelihood. " The sole use of money is to circulate consumable goods." " Money necessarily runs after goods, but goods do not always or necessarily run after money. The man who buys, does not always mean to sell again, but frequently to use or to consume ; whereas he who sells, always means to buy again. The one may frequently have done the whole, but the other can never have done more than the one-half of his business. It is not for its own sake that men desire money, but for the sake of what they can purchase with it." " The great wheel of circulation is altogether different from the goods which are circulated by means of it."

Adam Smith's vindication of Free Trade rests on this

conception of the functions of money, combined, as we remarked before, with his belief in the advantages of the division of labour. Through all the many chapters of his fourth book, in which with unwearying persistence he traces to their origin the varieties of fallacious reasoning used to support the "mean and malignant expedients" of the Mercantile System, the argument may be said to be based on this dual foundation. He has been reproached by recent writers for his 'cosmopolitan' attitude; and there can be no question that he held firmly the belief, and that he was instant in pressing it, that the advantages of the division of labour did not cease to be real when nations took the place of individuals as the figures in the industrial world, and that the fact that money was no more and no less than a convenient instrument of commerce, was not less but perhaps even more true an account of the matter, when the exchanging parties belonged, not to the same, but to different nations. "Were all nations," he writes, "to follow the liberal system of free exportation and free importation, the different states into which a great continent was divided would so far resemble the different provinces of a great empire."

The advantages of the division of labour, then, did not, in his opinion, cease with the geographical boundaries of a nation. Nations, like individuals, possessed different advantages, whether natural or acquired, whether derived from circumstances of situation, or soil, or climate, or based upon long practice or inherited aptitude, which fitted them to produce particular commodities. The division of labour between individual workmen, and trades, and districts, resulted in an increase of skill, and a saving of time; and similar results would follow on the division of labour between nations. Both parties would benefit by the free exchange

of the commodities which they were respectively better
fitted to produce.

The argument for Free Trade may be said still to rest in
part on a similar foundation to that on which Adam Smith
may be held to have thus implicitly, if not explicitly,
based his pleading. It might indeed be urged that the
analogy between nations and individuals is open to improvement and correction. It might be argued, and Adam
Smith himself recognised that there was some force in the
argument, that, so far as long practice or inherited aptitude
is the source of advantage, a policy which protected
struggling industries might enable a young country to attain
more surely the free independence of industrial maturity,
were the protection only removed at the proper moment.
And, on the other hand, it might be contended that the
possible drawbacks, which may attend the division of labour
between individuals, do not attach, at any rate in the same
manner or degree, to that between nations. The mere fact
of distance affords a kind of 'natural protection' to the
home producers of commodities which do not admit of easy
and cheap transportation from foreign countries; and a
nation can hardly be one-sided, or its work monotonous, in
the same way as an individual can.

But, whatever conclusion we may now form on the merits
of this part of Adam Smith's argument, which he may be
said to have himself urged implicitly rather than explicitly,[1]
there can be no question of the pertinency of the other
part to the controversies of our own time. The fact that
trade is essentially an exchange of goods for goods cannot,

[1] Colonel Torrens (1780 — 1864), who wrote several essays and
pamphlets on economic subjects, described international commerce as
the "territorial division of labour."

when once it is grasped, be seriously questioned; and the
conclusion which Adam Smith drew is inevitable, that a
nation must pay for its imports by its exports. The
method of payment might be, he admitted, obscure and
indirect, and the time of payment might be postponed.
But in the long run the goods which a nation imported from
foreign countries must be given and taken in exchange for
the goods which it exported. Part of those exports, as
part of those imports, might, it was true, take the form of
money or bullion; but, if a nation were like Great Britain,
and did not itself produce the precious metals in any
appreciable degree, it must have procured this money by
the previous export of other goods, and, in any event, the
movement of bullion was small compared with the transport of goods, and did not take place whenever it could be
conveniently avoided. A merchant "naturally" "exerts his
invention to find out a way of paying his foreign debts
rather by the exportation of commodities than by that of
gold and silver." '—

The Mercantile System, which Adam Smith assailed as
representative of the erroneous views which were then
current on money and foreign trade, has, it is true, been
somewhat misrepresented; and this misrepresentation is
partly due to his unsparing onslaught. Later inquiry has
shown that the system possessed some justification in the
circumstances amongst which it originated, and that it was
held in a more extravagant form by some of its irresponsible
supporters than its authors[1] would have sanctioned.
"Some" of the arguments advanced by its advocates were,
Adam Smith himself admits, "partly solid," though they

[1] Such as Thomas Mun and Sir Josiah Child, who wrote in the
seventeenth century.

were also "partly sophistical." Those advocates did not, for example, approve of positive restrictions on the exportation of gold and silver: they turned their attention rather to the 'balance of trade.' But the system does appear to have at least encouraged the notion that money was the main form of wealth, and that national riches consisted in the abundance of gold and silver; and it certainly countenanced the idea that a nation was not really prospering unless there was on the whole 'balance of trade' a greater flow of the precious metals into than out of it, that to secure this 'favourable' balance the exports of goods must be larger than the imports, and that therefore the former must be encouraged by bounties, and the latter discouraged by duties, though these must not be imposed on the raw materials needed in manufactures.

Adam Smith met these arguments by an appeal to the true functions of money, and the real nature of exchange. Money was a commodity, which, like every other commodity, would go where it was chiefly wanted, and all encouragement of its importation was as unnecessary as restrictions on its exportation would in the long run be futile. "A country that has wherewithal to buy gold and silver will never be in want of those metals," and, "on account of" their "small bulk and great value," "no commodities can be more easily transported from one place to another." The Mercantile System really defeated its own object; for, were a 'favourable' balance of trade secured for the time, and the exports rendered larger than the imports, the influx of bullion would tend to decrease its value, and to raise the prices of goods. This would tend to bring goods from abroad rather than money, to fetch the high prices, and to send money abroad rather than goods to the places where it was comparatively scarce, and therefore more valuable. Nor was money the most desirable form of wealth. "It would be too ridiculous to go about seriously to prove that wealth does not consist in money, or in gold or silver, but in what money purchases, and is valuable only for purchasing." "Gold and silver, whether in the shape of coin or of plate, are utensils, it must be remembered, as much as the furniture of the kitchen," and "to attempt to increase the wealth of any country, either by introducing or by detaining in it an unnecessary quantity of gold and silver, is as absurd as it would be to attempt to increase the good cheer of private families by obliging them to keep an unnecessary number of kitchen utensils."

On these points Adam Smith's reasoning is as pertinent as it was when it was first advanced. The Protectionist arguments of the present day are generally tainted with the same erroneous conception of money and trade as that which infected the Mercantile System, though they may conceal the taint even more skilfully. There is the same reluctance to admit that trade is essentially an exchange of goods for goods, that buying implies selling, that, if money be used, the man who sells goods for money really buys money with goods, and the man who buys goods with money really sells money for goods, that a nation after a similar fashion pays for its imports with its exports, that money forms an 'insignificant' part of these, and flows 'naturally' where it is wanted, and that a country which does not produce the precious metals must have procured them by the previous export of other commodities.

The facts are now, it is true, more obscure and complicated; and they are therefore more likely to engender confusion. England, for example, has a vast carrying trade,

D

and her shipping industry really constitutes a valuable
export of capital and labour. But it does not appear in the
statistics of exports, and yet a return for it must be made
in the imports. And, again, England has made, and continues to make, advances of capital to foreign countries.
This capital swells the exports when it goes out, and the
interest paid for it year by year swells the imports. And,
once more, the progress of manufacturing industry, the
improvement of means of transport, and the development
of financial organisation, have contributed to bring England
into commercial relations with all quarters of the world ;
and it may be the case that, as in Adam Smith's time, she
pays for the imports from one country by her exports to
another, or there may now be many more links in the chain
of connection. Such circumstances as these tend to obscure
the facts ; but they do not affect the substantial validity of
Adam Smith's argument, or the pertinency of its application
to the controversies of the present day.

CHAPTER II.

THOMAS ROBERT MALTHUS. 1766–1834.

THE PRINCIPLE OF POPULATION.

Malthus' Life—Origin of his *Essay*—Changes in the Second Edition—
His general Economic Opinions—The Distress of the Times—The
Poor Law—The Circumstances of English Agriculture—Argument
of the *Essay*—The Increase of Food—And of Men—The Three
Propositions—The Checks to Population, Positive and Preventive;
Vice, Misery, and Moral Restraint—The Character of Malthus'
Work—Relation of the *Essay* to Present Facts—The Law of
Diminishing Returns—Subsequent Changes—Malthus' own Position
—Contrasted with that of Recent Writers—The Checks to Popu-
lation—Malthus' Account of Moral Restraint—Bagehot's Criticism—
Malthus' own Position—Elasticity of the Standard of Comfort—
Physiological Considerations.

MALTHUS, who occupies the second place in historical
order among English economists, has been described as the
"best-abused man of the age." He has certainly suffered,
more than most men, from the misrepresentations of enemies
and friends; and both alike have often been content to
suppose rather than ascertain what he himself said. The
controversy which arose during his life has not yet been
closed; and now, as then, it is conducted with little reference to the language of the author whose views furnish the
ostensible subject of dispute. And yet the consultation of
Malthus' own writings would in many instances convict a

supporter of exaggeration and a critic of misunderstanding, while a due regard to the circumstances of his life, and the conditions under which his views were formed and expressed, might impose a salutary check on their indiscriminate adoption, at the same time as it prevented their wholesale condemnation.

Like Adam Smith, he was a product of his age and surroundings. His father, Daniel Malthus, was a friend, correspondent, and executor of Rousseau, and shared the French writer's belief in the perfectibility of man in a reformed state of society. He conducted the education of his sons on somewhat the same lines as those laid down in Rousseau's *Émile*, and he attempted to give free scope for the independent development of character. But we may believe that he also familiarised his children with the ideas which he had himself embraced, and that the future economist was bred in an atmosphere charged with visionary enthusiasm and fanciful hope. After an education, which was somewhat desultory, and was apparently imparted in his father's house until he reached the age of nine or ten, when he was sent, first to a small private school at Bath, and then to a larger one at Warrington kept by a clergyman who was, like his father, imbued with the educational theories of Rousseau, he proceeded to Jesus College, Cambridge, graduated as ninth wrangler in 1788, and in 1797 obtained a Fellowship. He then stayed for some time at his father's house at Albury in Surrey, and they discussed together the questions of the day.

But they approached the discussion from different standpoints, for Malthus had by this time shaken off the influence of his early training, and felt a decided reaction against it. He now assailed those French revolutionary doctrines which his father continued to advocate; and, in particular, he directed his assault against the new form of presentation¯ into which they had been thrown that very year in William Godwin's *Enquirer*.   The discussion led to the expression of his thoughts upon paper, and this to the publication in 1798 of an anonymous *Essay on the Principle of Population as it affects the Future Improvement of Society.*

This was the origin of his famous essay.   It was, as a critic has observed,[1] "an anonymous pamphlet in a political controversy"; and it had the faults of a controversial pamphlet.   "Its main fault," as the same critic has said, "was not incompleteness but wrongness of emphasis."   As Malthus himself remarked at a later time, "having found the bow bent too much one way," he was perhaps "induced to bend it too much the other in order to make it straight." And so the second edition of the essay, which was published in 1803, differed considerably from the first.   He states in the preface that he had "endeavoured to soften some of the harshest conclusions of the first essay," and that "in its present shape it may be considered as a new work."   In the interval he had travelled abroad.   In 1799 he had visited Germany, Sweden, Norway, Finland and Russia, and on his return he had written a pamphlet on the *High Price of Provisions*, in which he had spoken of a second edition of his essay.   But, before he fulfilled his promise, he had seized the opportunity, which was afforded by the temporary interruption of war consequent on the Peace of Amiens, to visit France and Switzerland; and the second edition of the essay comprised a great mass of detailed evidence, much of which had been obtained, or at any rate tested, by his own personal observation and

[1] Mr. Bonar in his *Malthus and his Work*, p. 5.

inquiry. The title was altered, and it now ran : *An Essay on the Principle of Population, or a View of its Past and Present Effects on Human Happiness.* Before it had been mainly controversial, and intended to refute those visions of a future state of ideal perfection which had been entertained by writers like Godwin in England, and Condorcet in France, who either did not notice at all the principle of population, or else treated it " very lightly," and represented the " difficulties arising from it as at a great and almost immeasurable distance." Now it was chiefly statistical, and consisted for the most part of a review of the history of the past and the conditions of the present.

, From this time onwards Malthus devoted his studies and energies especially to the repeated examination and amended expression of what he held to be the truth on the question of population, and, in a subordinate degree, to the investigation of the other branches of political economy. He issued six editions of the essay during his life, and he was continually making additions and corrections. The general result of these changes is that his attitude on the whole matter is far from being so extreme as his supporters and opponents have often imagined ; and here, as in his other contributions to economic inquiry, he inclines to a middle view. He opposed the abstract reasoning on economic subjects of his contemporary Ricardo ; and that economist states, in one of his letters to Malthus, that, if he himself was " too theoretical" (which he " really " believed, " was the case "), Malthus, on the other hand, was, he thought, " too practical." Hence it was that in his writings on general economics Malthus appears to have anticipated many of the charges, which have more recently been brought by adherents of the ' historical ' against the ' abstract deductive ' method of inquiry;[1] and that his unorthodox views on some points, such as the advisability of a moderate amount of protection, and the danger of a general glut of goods, indicate at once his steady resolve to allow weight to practical exigencies, and his inclination to adopt the view which seemed the more moderate and humane.

His general economic writings consist of the tract on *The High Price of Provisions*, which was published in 1800, his *Observations on the Corn Laws*, which were published in 1814, his *Grounds of an Opinion on the Policy of Restricting Importation*, of the same date, his *Nature and Progress of Rent*, of the following year, his *Principles of Political Economy*, published in 1820, his *Measure of Value*, published in 1823, and his *Definitions in Political Economy*, published in 1827. But it is not by these writings, but by his *Essay on Population*, that he is now remembered ; and it was that which originally made him famous. In 1805 he was appointed Professor of History and Political Economy in the East India College at Haileybury, and he continued to hold this post until his death. In 1819 he was elected a Fellow of the Royal Society, in 1821 he joined in founding the London Political Economy Club and, in 1834, the London Statistical Society. At the end of this year he died suddenly of disease of the heart; and he is buried in Bath Abbey, where his epitaph states that he was "one of the best men and truest philosophers of any age or country, raised by native dignity of mind above the misrepresentations of the ignorant and the neglect of the great." This description seems to be something more than the natural, but exaggerated, eulogy of mourning relatives and friends ; for Mackintosh, who was his colleague at Haileybury, is reported to have said : "I have known

---

[1] See chap. v. below.

Adam Smith slightly, Ricardo well, Malthus intimately. Is it not something to say for a science that its three great masters were about the three best men I ever knew?"

The character of the Essay on Population was, as we have seen, partly due to the immediate personal surroundings of the author. Malthus was brought up in the midst of what he thought were delusions, and he made a vigorous attempt to disprove them by showing that there was a "cause intimately united with the very nature of man," the effects of which would be fatal to the continuance of a society based, as Godwin had urged, on equality. But the conditions of the times in which he lived also exercised an influence on his writings. His father's dreams of the universal prevalence of happiness in an ideal society had been originally formed before the French Revolution, and his life closed with the century. But Malthus himself wrote at a time when the practical illustration of revolutionary ideas furnished in France was filling men's minds with consternation and abhorrence. In England the political outlook was gloomy, and the economic position distressing. The reaction caused by the cruel and violent excesses of the French Revolution combined with the absorbing interest of the War to arrest the progress of legislative reform, and the oppressive burden of taxation entailed by military expenditure was increased by the sufferings attendant on a succession of bad harvests. The average income received by the labourer was as much below what it is now as the prices of the ordinary and necessary articles of his consumption were above their present level. The financial ways and means of the war were provided, in a very considerable degree, by England alone; and it is estimated that the yearly interest on the debt which was, to a large extent, incurred in consequence, amounted in the end to as much as a tenth of the income of the nation, and the total taxes to a fifth. The bad harvests sent up the price of wheat to very high figures, and on one occasion, in 1801, to a hundred and eighty shillings a quarter. Starvation was not merely threatened, but occurred ; and it was accompanied, or preceded, by disease. In 1795, three years before the publication of Malthus' essay, the Government had recourse to Coercion Acts to restrain the distressed 'lower orders' from rising, and a mob crying out for 'bread' stopped the king's carriage in the streets.

The distress was real and urgent ; but the remedy which was proposed was calculated to effect a temporary and delusive amelioration at the cost of permanent and increasing mischief. The Poor Law was to be modified in the direction of greater laxity ; but the lax administration of that law was already producing evil results. It tended to benefit the idle at the expense of the industrious by the indiscriminate manner in which relief was given. The evils thus occasioned by the administration of the law reached their climax before its reform in 1834 ; but the whole period extending from about 1750 to that date was a period of increasing laxity and mischief. By its close the growth of the rates had become nothing less than appalling. The independence of the labourer had sustained serious and abiding injury. Farmers were compelled to dismiss the thrifty and industrious to make room for the lazy and thriftless, whom the parish forced them to employ ; and they were enabled to reduce the wages which they paid themselves, and to supply the deficiencies by parish 'allowances' out of the pockets of the ratepayers. The Royal Commission, which was appointed to inquire into the working of the unreformed Poor Law, found that in one place the weekly wages of a pauper were higher than those of independent labourers; at another that women complained of the refusal of their husbands to improve their position by seeking the status of paupers; and at a third that the owners of the land offered the whole of it to the assembled paupers for the simple reason that the rates exceeded the rents. It was especially in the south of England that this indiscriminate method of relief was carried to excess, and it is there that the recovery from its mischievous consequences has been most difficult and gradual.

The administration of the Poor Law had undergone some relaxation a little while before Malthus wrote, for in 1782 Gilbert's Act had abolished the workhouse test of destitution, and the guardians were positively prohibited from sending to it any but the 'impotent,' and in 1795 the demoralising system of 'allowances' in aid of wages had been introduced at a meeting of Berkshire magistrates at Speenhamland.

This relaxation of the old stringency had apparently begun to produce some of those effects which by 1834 had attained their climax. The first half of the century had been marked by a rise in wages, and by scarcely any increase in population. The domestic system of industry had combined with the unwillingness of landlords to build cottages on their estates, for fear that the occupants might establish a 'settlement,' and eventually become chargeable upon the rates, to postpone the age at which a man would leave his father or master, and take a wife to keep house for himself. But the middle of the century had coincided with the commencement of a series of important inventions, which produced a 'revolution' in the character and methods of industry. Adam Smith had lived on the eve of that revolution;

or at any rate he had seen little more than the first faint
streaks of light which indicate the approach of day.   But
Malthus saw its development.   Trade began to leave the
small domestic establishments of the country villages, and
to pass to the large new factories of the growing towns.
Many fresh openings of gaining a living appeared, and men
hastened the time of their marriage, and were more disposed
to trust to fortune to provide the means of livelihood.   The
war with France gave an added intensity to the demand for
men which the new factories had started, and the policy of
the landlords and the ruling classes was reversed.   The
interests of the nation, and the duty of the individual, were
held to lie in the encouragement of population, and the
erection of cottages proceeded side by side with growing
laxity in the administration of the Poor Law.   The more
children a man had, the greater was considered to be
his claim to parish allowance, and relief was to be made
"a matter of right and honour, instead of a ground for
opprobrium and contempt."

But there was no more food to fill the new mouths which
were thus coming into existence.   Bread was growing
dearer, apart even from deficient harvests, and wheat was
being raised from land which yielded no more than eight
bushels to the acre.   Nor could it then be freely imported
from abroad owing to the restrictions of the Corn Laws;
and the opinion of Adam Smith that the restoration of the
entire freedom of trade in Great Britain was as visionary
as the realisation of an Utopia did not as yet appear likely
to be proved mistaken.   Malthus himself declared that a
"perfect freedom of trade" was "a vision which it" was
"to be feared" could "never be realised."

Whatever hopes might, then, be formed by imaginative

enthusiasts of the happiness of the future, it was impossible to ignore the actual misery of the present; and, so far as the views of Malthus are extravagant or erroneous, the error and extravagance may be largely ascribed to the liability, from which few men are free, to generalise unduly from the circumstances of his own times. The niggard-liness of nature and the fecundity of man were two most obvious facts of the times; and it is little wonder that, in his eagerness to controvert the Utopian position of Godwin, Malthus should give exaggerated expression to those facts.

In his statement of the first he affirms an important econo-mic theory. He must have noticed that in England cultivation was advancing from the richer land to the poorer land, which only yielded eight bushels an acre; and he would conclude that this was due to the fact that, while the demand for food required an increased production, farmers found that the richer land did not continue to yield the same or increased returns to each successive application of capital and labour to its cultivation, and that, if more food were wanted, it must be obtained with greater expenditure of capital and labour from the richer land, or they must turn to the poorer land. The law of *diminishing returns*, to use the technical language of economic science, was in operation, and the bounty of nature was limited. Malthus did not state this law in any very exact form, but he seems to have possessed on the whole a correct conception of it. He says that, "when acre has been added to acre till all the fertile land is occupied, the yearly increase of food must depend upon the melioration of the land already in possession. This is a fund which, from the nature of all soils, instead of increasing, must be gradually diminishing." [1]

---

[1] The quotations are made from the sixth edition of the Essay.

From the consideration of the law determining the increase of food he turned to look at the growth in the numbers of man. He examined the "effects of one great cause intimately united with the very nature of man," which had "been constantly and powerfully operating since the commencement of society." This was the "constant tendency in all animated life to increase beyond the nourishment prepared for it." If the "germs of existence contained in this earth," he remarks, "could freely develop themselves," they "would fill millions of worlds in the course of a few thousand years." But the tendency was, in the last resource, held in check by "necessity, that imperious, all-pervading law of nature," and, in the case of man, necessity was reinforced by reason. "In no state that we have yet known," he observes, "has the power of population been left to exert itself with perfect freedom." But "in the northern states of America, where the means of subsistence have been more ample, the manners of the people more pure, and the checks to early marriages fewer, than in any of the modern states of Europe, the population has been found to double itself, for above a century and a half successively, in less than twenty-five years," and in "the back settlements" in fifteen years. Euler had calculated the period of doubling at twelve years and four-fifths, and Sir William Petty at ten years. But, "to be perfectly sure" that he is "far within the truth," Malthus himself takes "the slowest of these rates of increase"; and, with a fondness for mathematics which might have been pardoned in a Cambridge wrangler, he contrasts the increase of population, "when unchecked," with the "supposed" increase of the productions of the earth, which, he admits, is "not so easy to determine," by com-

paring the former to an increase in a "geometrical," and
the latter to one in an "arithmetical ratio."

He was more fully aware than some of his critics have
imagined that the analogy did not admit of exact application ; and he regarded it rather as indicating the extreme
limits set on either side by the minimum rate of increase
of population and the maximum rate of increase of food.
It was, he thought, conceivable that the supply of food in
England might be increased in the next and each succeeding twenty-five years, "by a quantity equal to what it
at present" produced, and "the most enthusiastic specu-
lator" could not "suppose a greater increase than this."
But on the other hand it might "safely be pronounced "—
and this calculation would be based on the "slowest" of the
"rates of increase "—"that population, when unchecked,"
would go "on doubling itself every twenty-five years."

Nor, again, did he fail to anticipate some of the objections of the critics, who have in his own day, and since
his death, attacked his essay, by the distinction he is always
careful to draw between the possible and the actual increase
of population. There were, in fact, three propositions which
he "intended" to prove. The first was that "population"
was "necessarily limited by the means of subsistence."
The second that "population invariably increases where
the means of subsistence increase, unless prevented by some
very powerful and obvious checks." And the third and
last that "these checks, and the checks which repress the
superior power of population, and keep its effects on a
level with the means of subsistence, are all resolvable into
moral restraint, vice, and misery." "The first of these
propositions," he states, "scarcely needs illustration." The
"second and third" were to be "sufficiently established by

a review of the immediate checks to population in the past and present state of society."

It is this review which occupies by far the larger part of the essay. It contains a great abundance of facts extracted from the records of travellers, or based upon personal investigation. Beginning with the "lowest stage of human society," he examines the conditions of the American Indians, the South Sea Islanders, the inhabitants of different parts of Africa, Siberia, the Turkish dominions and Persia, Indostan and Tibet, China and Japan, ancient Greece, Rome, and Northern Europe. He then passes in his second book to more modern times, and more civilised nations ; and here he has the assistance of "registers of births, deaths, and marriages," and makes abundant use of statistical calculations. He reviews successively the checks to population in Norway, Sweden, Russia, the middle parts of Europe, Switzerland, France, England, Scotland, and Ireland. The third book is devoted to an examination of the "different systems or expedients which have been proposed or have prevailed in society, as they affect the evils arising from the principle of population"; and, amongst these, he considers those schemes of social equality propounded by Godwin and Condorcet which had originally furnished the occasion for writing the essay, and emigration and the poor laws. In his fourth and final book he investigates the "prospects of the future" "respecting the removal or mitigation of the evils arising from the principle of population."

The checks to population are classified by him under two heads, of which the "positive" checks cut off an existing population, and the "preventive" hinder a population from coming into existence. A triple cross-division is also made, and the checks "are all resolvable into moral restraint, vice, and misery." As we pass from lower to higher stages of life and degrees of civilisation, the positive checks give place in prominence to the preventive ; and the same process is marked by an increasing predominance of moral restraint over vice and misery. Of the positive checks some, like famine and disease, are due to "laws of nature," and "may be called exclusively misery," and some "we obviously bring upon ourselves, such as wars, excesses, and many others which it would be in our power to avoid." "They are brought upon us by vice, and their consequences are misery." "The preventive check," on the other hand, "as far as it is voluntary, is peculiar to man, and arises from that distinctive superiority in his reasoning faculties which enables him to calculate distant consequences." It sometimes takes the form of vice, and sometimes of moral restraint.

The argument of which a summary account has just been given is more original in the manner of its presentation than in the foundation on which it rests. Malthus himself says that in the course of the "historical examination," which he made between his first and second editions, he found that "much more had been done" on the subject than he "had been aware of when" he "first published the essay." "The poverty and misery arising from a too rapid increase of population had been distinctly seen, and the most violent remedies proposed, so long ago as the times of Plato and Aristotle ;" and of "late years" the subject had been "treated" "by some of the French economists, occasionally by Montesquieu," and "among our own writers by Dr. Franklin, Sir JAMES STEWART, Mr. Arthur Young, and Mr. Townsend," in addition to those authors, " Hume, Wallace, Adam Smith, and Dr. Price," "from whose writings" he "had" directly "deduced the principle which formed the main argument of" his "essay." What he claimed to have done himself, was to state with greater "force and precision" "the comparison between the increase of population and food," to inquire "into the various modes by which" "population" was "kept down to the level of the means of subsistence," to pursue "the principle" "to its consequences," and to draw "practical inferences from it." But, as in the case of Adam Smith and his predecessors, it is to Malthus that the economic conception of the bearings of the principle is really due and he has stated it in such a way that his treatment may be regarded as substantially original. In his case, again, as in that of Adam Smith, the progress of economic inquiry has tended to modify and supplement his statement; and we may now proceed to consider the relation of his essay to the facts of the present day, viewed in the light of subsequent economic investigation.

The conception which he seems to have formed of the law of diminishing returns is, in the main, correct; but he does not lay stress, at any rate with sufficient explicitness, on the limiting conditions of its application to fact. The law of diminishing returns is the statement of a tendency which may be counteracted by opposing tendencies. It asserts that, after a certain point has been reached in the cultivation of land, the returns to each additional application of capital and labour will tend, other things being unaltered, not to increase proportionally to the increase of capital and labour. But it is difficult to fix the point with precision; and other things may not continue unaltered. It is possible that an increase of population may, while it augments the demand for food, permit of

E

more systematic organisation and greater division of labour
in raising it, and the consequence may be that an additional
application of labour to the cultivation of land may result
in a return which increases instead of diminishing.   And it
is also possible that such an improved method of cultivation
may follow on the application of additional capital in the
form of manures or mechanical appliances as to produce
an increasing and not a diminishing return.   It is possible,
again, that poorer soils may be taken into cultivation before
richer, because the initial application of capital and labour
required in the case of the latter, in the shape of draining
or fencing or the like, is greater than it is in that of the
former, or for some other reason ; and then, in the progress
of society, this initial application once accomplished, the
returns may become proportionally greater and not less.
Or, once more, it is possible that land may be applied to
different uses, or sown with different crops, in a more
advanced stage of civilisation; and then, while the returns
from the old use or the old crops might diminish, those
from the new may increase.

All these possibilities have to some extent been realised
in England since Malthus wrote.   A larger population has
permitted of more systematic organisation, and greater
division of labour, in manufactures, if not in agriculture ;
and the repeal of the Corn Laws has allowed the exchange
of the increased products of English manufacturing skill
and industry for more abundant supplies of foreign corn.
It has extended the number and area of the sources from
which food is provided for the population of England until
they embrace the wheat-fields of America, Russia, and India.
It has brought the rich virgin soils of the New World to
reinforce the more exhausted soils of the Old ; and it has

allowed some of these soils to be turned to other uses, and sown with other crops. The means of communication at home, and of transportation from abroad, have been vastly improved ; and the cost of conveying the produce to the market, which forms part of the total cost of production, has been considerably diminished. The methods of cultivation have undergone improvement ; and the close of the last, and the first half of the present, century saw a transformation in English agricultural practice which almost kept pace with the revolutionising inventions in manufacturing industry, while the period which followed on the repeal of the Corn Laws, and the introduction of Free Trade, was a period of high intensive farming unknown before.

It would be incorrect to say that Malthus ignored the effects which might be produced by such changes as these ; but he certainly could not have foreseen the full extent of their consequences. He was aware that there were "many parts of the globe" "hitherto uncultivated and almost unoccupied "; but the "process of improving" the "minds and directing" the "industry" of the inhabitants of "these thinly-peopled regions," " would," he thought, "be necessarily slow." He recognised that "Europe" was "by no means so fully peopled as it might be," that the "science of agriculture" had "been much studied in England and Scotland," and that there was "still a great portion of un-cultivated land in these countries." He speaks of the "employment of a larger capital in draining," or in applying "natural and artificial manures," as being "productive in a high degree" ; and he says that "an improved system of cultivation, and the use of better instruments, may for a long period more than counterbalance the tendency" to "smaller proportionate returns." "I can easily conceive," he writes, " that this country, with a proper direction of the national industry, might in the course of some centuries contain two or three times its present population : and yet every man in the kingdom be much better fed and clothed than he is at present." But he held that to allow " that by the best possible policy, and great encouragements to agriculture, the average produce of the island " of Great Britain " could be doubled in " " twenty-five years," would be " allowing, probably, a greater increase than could with reason be expected " ; and that " to suppose " that " in the next twenty-five years" it "could be quadrupled " would be " impossible," and " contrary to all our knowledge of the properties of land."

He was so far from being a pessimist that he believed that the pressure of population stimulated improvement. " Evil exists," he writes, " not to create despair, but activity " ; and he maintains that an increase of population is " both a great positive good and absolutely necessary to a further increase in the annual produce of the land and labour ot any country," " when it follows in its natural order." " It is an utter misconception of my argument," he says, " to infer that I am an enemy to population." " I am only an enemy to vice and misery." And he states that " a careful distinction should always be made between a redundant population and a population actually great."

But still · he was in a sense, as a French economist [1] has observed, no " geographer "; and, while he recognised the advantages of foreign commerce, he could not have anticipated the expansion and diffusion of English trade which would follow on the abandonment of a protectionist policy, and the provision of easy, inexpensive, and

[1] M. Leroy-Beaulieu.

rapid means of transportation. "In the wildness of speculation," he writes, "it has been suggested (of course more
in jest than in earnest) that Europe ought to grow its corn
in America, and devote itself solely to manufactures and
commerce, as the best sort of division of the labour of the
globe." Nor could he have gauged the dimensions to
which the tide of emigration of labour (or of capital) would
swell; and it was partly for this reason perhaps that he
regarded emigration as a "slight palliative" rather than an
"adequate remedy." "As a partial and temporary expedient,
and with a view to the more general cultivation of the earth
and the wider extension of civilisation," he thought that it
was "both useful and proper."

But probably the chief reason was that he conceived the
whole situation somewhat differently than we now do. He
appears to have regarded population as getting, now and
again, the start of improvement, and straining every nerve
to maintain an advantage in the race. We should perhaps
be inclined to be more positive in representing improvement
as, on the whole, in civilised countries keeping ahead of
population. "Though the barriers," he writes, "to a
further increase of population be not so well defined, and
so open to common observation, on continents as on islands,
yet they still present obstacles that are nearly as insur-
mountable, and the emigrant, impatient of the distresses
which he feels in his own country, is by no means secure of
finding relief in another. There is probably no island yet
known, the produce of which could not be further increased.
This is all that can be said of the whole earth. Both are
peopled up to their actual produce." In another passage
he remarks—"When we refer " " to the practical limits of
population, it is of great importance to recollect that they

must be always very far short of the utmost power of the
earth to produce food"; and it is "also of great importance
to recollect that long before this practical limit is obtained
in any country the rate of the increase of population will
gradually diminish."   On the whole we may probably
affirm that, although he remarked himself, when writing on
the determining influence of population, and answering the
question whether agriculture might "with more propriety
be termed the efficient cause of population, than population
of agriculture," that "all the prejudices respecting population" had "perhaps arisen from a mistake about the order
of precedence," yet the course of later inquiry has tended
to throw some doubt upon his own entire freedom from
mistakes about that order.   His perception of the elastic
nature of the limit set by the law of diminishing returns
might now be regarded as dim and imperfect by comparison
with our more extensive and positive knowledge ; and he
confined his considerations for the most part to agricultural
industry.   We should be inclined to lay greater stress on
the elasticity of the limit, and to set the tendency to
increasing returns in English manufactures against the
tendency to diminishing returns in our agriculture, and to
returns which perhaps increase, and perhaps are at present
constant, but as yet are scarcely diminishing, in the agriculture of the countries which supply us with wheat.   But
it must, on the other hand, be remembered that he thought
that to allow "the produce of the earth to be absolutely
unlimited, scarcely" removed "the weight of a hair from"
his "argument, which" depended "entirely upon the
differently increasing ratios of population and food"; and
that subsequent experience has so far tended to support his
position that it has witnessed in our own country an increase

in the average produce of wheat from twenty-three bushels an acre in 1770 to twenty-eight in 1880, and a simultaneous growth in population from some six to thirty-five millions.[1]

If we now turn to the other part of his argument, we may say that he was on the whole perhaps inclined to lay greater stress on the tendency of population to increase than on the strength of those "positive and preventive checks" which he illustrated with such abundant detail. "In every country," he writes, "some of these checks are, with more or less force, in constant operation; yet, notwithstanding their general prevalence, there are few states in which there is not a constant effort in the population to increase beyond the means of subsistence. This constant effort as constantly tends to subject the lower classes of society to distress, and to prevent any great permanent amelioration of their condition." In the first edition of his essay he had represented these checks to population as two in number—vice and misery; and it was only in his second edition that he recognised the "action of another check," consisting in "moral restraint."

He is very careful to indicate what he means by this. He defines it as a "restraint from marriage from prudential motives with a conduct strictly moral during the period of this restraint"; and no authority can be found in his writings for what is known as Neo-Malthusianism. It is one of the many examples of the irony of fate to which he has been a victim that his name should be thus employed; for he expressly states that a "cause which may prevent any particular evil may be beyond all comparison worse than the evil itself," and in another passage he writes, "I should be extremely sorry to say anything which could

[1] Cf. Bonar's *Malthus and his Work*, p. 69.

either directly or remotely be construed unfavourably to the cause of virtue." Nor again did he wish, as some of his critics have thought, to propose "a law to prohibit the poor from marrying." He sought, simply and solely, to impress upon us "our obligation not to marry till we have a fair prospect of being able to support our children," and he argued that time should be allowed "for forming those strong and lasting attachments without which the married state is generally more productive of misery than of happiness." "It is less the object of the present work," he writes, "to propose new plans of improving society than to inculcate the necessity of resting content with that mode of improvement which already has in part been enacted upon as dictated by the course of nature, and of not obstructing the advances which would otherwise be made in this way."

Bagehot has epigrammatically remarked [1] that "in its first form the *Essay on Population* was conclusive as an argument, only it was based on untrue facts; in its second form it was based on true facts, but it was inconclusive as an argument." For, he urges, by introducing this additional check of moral restraint Malthus "has cut away the ground of his whole argument. If there be this principle of virtuous self-restraint, he no longer answers Godwin; he no longer destroys the dreams of perfectibility. If it be possible for a perfectly virtuous community to limit their numbers, they will perform that duty just as they perform all others; there is no infallible principle that will break up the village community; it can adjust its numbers to its food, and may last for ever."

Here, as elsewhere, Malthus seems to have possessed a dim perception rather than a clear vision of the full con-

[1] *Economic Studies*, p. 137.

sequences of his statements.   His argument, indeed, even
in its amended form, was fatal to systems of equality, but
it was not fatal to progress; and he appears, though
imperfectly, to have discerned this fact.   " Universally," he
writes, ''the practice of mankind on the subject of marriage
has been much superior to their theories; and however
frequent may have been the declamations on the duty of
entering into this state," "each individual has practically
found it necessary to consider of the means of supporting
a family before he ventured to take so important a step.
That great *vis medicatrix reipublicæ*, the desire of bettering
our condition and the fear of making it worse, has been
constantly in action, and has been constantly directing
people into the right road in spite of all the declamations
which tended to lead them aside.   Owing to this powerful
spring of health in every state, which is nothing more than
an inference from the general course of the laws of nature
irresistibly forced on each man's attention, the prudential
check to marriage has increased in Europe, and it cannot
be unreasonable to conclude that it will still make further
advances."

But, on the other hand, there are passages which seem to
show that he never rid himself entirely of the associations
of his first edition.   He "was accused," so he states
himself, "of not allowing sufficient weight " in his "review
of the different stages of society" to "moral restraint"; but
he "thought that" he should "not be found to have erred
much" on that account.   He was not disposed to deny that
the sexual passion was "one of the principal ingredients of
human happiness," and that its "extinction or diminution"
"would probably convert human life either into a cold and
cheerless blank or a scene of savage and merciless ferocity."

It was, therefore, "regulation and direction" that "were wanted, not diminution or extinction." But he believed that "few" of his "readers" could "be less sanguine" than himself "in their expectations of any sudden and great change in the general conduct of men on this subject." And, firmly as he held the opinion that the " system of the poor laws" was the "first grand obstacle" which opposed the accomplishment of such a change, and emphatically as he declared that that system had "been justly stated to be an evil, in comparison of which the national debt, with all its magnitude of terror," was "of little moment," he still felt that the "evil" was "now so deeply seated, and the relief given by the poor laws so widely extended, that no man of humanity could venture to propose their immediate abolition." He himself "would never wish to push general principles too far," and he only proposed "the *gradual*, and *very gradual*, abolition of the poor laws."

Nor, again, did he form any very definite or consistent conception of the considerations which entered into the thoughts of the man who practised moral restraint. Sometimes he writes as if they were confined to the provision of the means requisite to secure the necessaries of a bare subsistence. Sometimes he includes considerations of rank and social status for the man himself and of education for his children. "The comforts of the lower classes of society," he writes in one passage, "do not depend solely upon food, nor even upon strict necessaries." And in another he says that "two or three steps of descent in society, particularly at this round of the ladder where education ends and ignorance begins, will not be considered by the generality of people as a chimerical but a real evil."

To this side of Malthus' argument, as to that connected

with the increase of food, later economic inquiry has added an element of elasticity which is more prominent than it seems to be on his pages. It is now stated with greater emphasis than he can be said to have employed, that the 'standard of comfort,' which under the form of 'moral restraint' exercises an influence on marriage and the rearing of children, is not limited to the physical minimum of a bare existence, but is based on a moral minimum of decencies, comforts, and luxuries, below which men or women will not willingly sink, by incurring the expense attendant on marriage. The standard may vary from class to class, and from country to country; and it may be, and as a matter of fact it has been, raised from age to age, and generation to generation. The element of food no longer enters so largely as it once did into the component parts of the standard in a civilised and progressive country like England, and the marriage rate conforms rather to the general fluctuations of trade, with its alternating periods of prosperity and depression, than, as it once seemed to do, to the rise and fall of the price of wheat. The 'iron' law of wages, which is represented by some socialist writers as ever forcing wages down to the level of a bare subsistence, and by others as tending to make them conform to the requirements of the standard of comfort, because, if they rise above this level, population will grow and competition for employment increase, loses much, if not all, of its hard and unyielding character when subjected to the test of the modern interpretation of the standard.

This emphatic recognition of the elastic nature of the standard of comfort is an important modification which has been introduced into Malthus' reasoning by later economic study; but that study has only served to confirm, though some of its exponents have treated the confirmation as a fresh discovery, the truth of his observation that " even poverty itself, which appears to be the great spur to industry, when it has once passed certain limits, almost ceases to operate." A 'degradation of labour' may follow on some very serious and extensive economic calamity, before which the restorative influence of the standard of comfort is powerless; and in the same way it has been urged that it needs a long spell of a considerable increase in wages to elevate that standard. The standard, in short, offers resistance to change; but it cannot prevail against the influence of a sudden change of great magnitude, or a gradual change of a persistent character.

Another important commentary on Malthus' Essay, which subsequent study has brought into prominence, is suggested by the reflection that we have not yet arrived at a full knowledge of the physiological laws which govern the increase of population. There may be relations between the nervous strain, which often accompanies a higher standard of material comfort and intellectual acquirements, and the growth of population, which have not yet been completely disclosed or investigated. But, whether the explanation of changes in the rate at which population increases rests on a moral or a physiological basis, the tendency of present economic thought seems on the whole to incline slightly in the opposite direction to that imposed by Malthus on the thought of his own day. He wrote especially for his own time, and he generalised, perhaps unduly, from the facts he was himself witnessing. The practical success he immediately achieved combines with the important and painstaking nature of his inquiries to give him a high place among English economists.

CHAPTER III.

DAVID RICARDO. 1772—1823.

THE THEORY OF RENT.

The 'Industrial Revolution' of the Eighteenth Century—Ricardo's
Assumption of Competition—His Influence on Economic Opinion—
His Jewish Nationality, and his Training on the Stock Exchange—
His Writings—Their Abstract Character—Their Misrepresentation
by other Writers—Marx's Theory of Surplus Value—Ricardo's
Theory of Rent—Origin of the Theory—Its Statement by Ricardo—
Definition of Rent—Its Origin and Growth—Ricardo's want of
Systematic Arrangement—Conclusions Drawn by him from the
Theory : (1) The Connection of Rent with Price—(2) Erroneous
Opinions of other Writers—(3) The Order of Distribution of Wealth
and the Progress of Society—Subsequent Criticism—The Historical
Order of Cultivation—The Theory must be Interpreted Liberally—
The Assumption of Competition—The 'No-rent' Land—The Un-
earned Increment—Difficulty of distinguishing it.

THE close of the last and the beginning of the present
century mark a period of momentous importance in English
industrial history. The character and methods of industry
then underwent a change of so vast a nature as to earn the
name of a ' revolution.' It was on the eve of this change
that Adam Smith wrote the *Wealth of Nations ;* but
Malthus saw its fulfilment, and he was contemporary with
RICARDO, the third of the great writers who are known by
the common designation of the ' older English economists.'

This ' industrial revolution ' transformed the character of

agriculture, manufactures, and commerce. The system of
large holdings of land tended to supersede the small
scattered holdings of the past; and the open fields and
wastes were rapidly enclosed. Cultivation conducted on
scientific principles was substituted for primitive methods.
The breeding of cattle was improved, and a new order of
rotation of crops introduced.

But the changes in manufacturing industry were more
revolutionary. A series of inventions, consisting of the water-
frame, the spinning-jenny, the self-acting mule, and, finally,
the power-loom, summoned into activity the cotton industry,
which was eventually to supersede the woollen trade as
the chief textile industry of the country, and to render
parts of Lancashire as populous as London itself. The
process of smelting iron by coal revived the declining
energy of the iron trade, and attracted it to the neighbour-
hood of the collieries of the North and the Midlands.
The construction of canals improved the means of communication between the growing industrial centres; and, some
years later, the roads of Telford and Macadam took the
place of those "vile" and "execrable" highways, which had
excited the indignation of ARTHUR YOUNG on his travels at
the beginning of this period in the middle of the eighteenth
century. But it was the invention of the steam-engine which,
more than anything else, caused the 'revolution' in manufacturing industry. It gave an added significance to the
mechanical improvements which were introduced into the
cotton trade; it was applied to blast-furnaces in the iron
industry; and, finally, it tended to supersede the canal and
the road by the railway.

These various improvements were not fully accomplished
until the middle of the present century; but the changes

which they occasioned in the character and methods of industry and commerce were taking place during Ricardo's life. There had been some examples of capitalistic undertakings even of the present type [1] before the 'industrial revolution'; but they had formed the exceptions to a general rule. But now the small domestic establishments of the country gave way to the large factories of the towns. The craftsman, who worked together with his apprentices and journeymen, was superseded by the employer who might not know the faces of his workmen, just as in agriculture the farmers became more distinct from the labourers. The familiar routine of a neighbouring market, where fashion varied gradually and slightly, and goods were produced to order, was exchanged for the feverish activity and fluctuating demands of trade with distant places and strange customers.

The age was one of 'revolution,' and, it almost seemed, of anarchy, in industrial affairs. Population increased with rapidity, and commerce and manufactures expanded; and the great war with France gave additional stimulus to both, to be followed by a distressing depression in trade and agriculture after the conclusion of peace. The war promoted the growth of population; for men were required by the recruiting officer as well as the employer, to fill the ranks of the army as well as to occupy places in the factories, and it was regarded as a patriotic duty to increase the numbers of the nation. And the war also encouraged the development of manufactures, and advanced the prosperity of agriculture. It raised the price of English corn, and it opened

---

[1] The owners of actual *factories* should be distinguished from the "*undertakers*" (cf. p. 6), who in many cases seem to have supplied the materials, and sometimes the implements, of industry to the small domestic "*manufacturers*," and sold the finished goods.

markets abroad to English goods, by suspending the industry of the Continental nations. This expansion of trade, like the growth of population, was accompanied by new and significant circumstances. The population moved from one place to another, from the villages into the towns ; and the trade was subject to sudden and considerable fluctuations, and apprentices and workmen were liable to speedy dismissal if the demand for the goods which they produced abated. A busy, restless competition, with men, women, and children, hurrying themselves, or hurried by others, in new and different directions, and factories crowded with hands, and working at full pressure, seemed to prevail.

Such was the condition of the industrial world of England when, in 1817, two years after the conclusion of peace, Ricardo published his *Principles of Political Economy and Taxation.* In basing his reasoning on the universal prevalence of competition, he seems to have formed a conception of society which did not differ widely from the actual circumstances of English industry at the time. He appeared to have arranged the seeming anarchy of affairs in the intelligible order of so luminous and precise a theory of the action of competition that the success of his book was immediate and complete. His friend and contemporary Malthus thought indeed that "the main part of his structure would not stand"; and Malthus' successor at Haileybury, RICHARD JONES (1790—1855), controverted many of Ricardo's positions on the theory of rent in his *Essay on the Distribution of Wealth and on the Sources of Taxation.* But Ricardo's influence on the general course of English economic opinion remained unshaken. JAMES MILL, who had been his intimate friend, and, according to Bentham, who said, " I was the spiritual father of Mill, and

Mill was the spiritual father of Ricardo," the real inspirer
of his opinions, published a treatise on the *Elements
of Political Economy*, in 1821, in which he presented the
Ricardian theories in a neat and compact form. J. R.
McCULLOCH (1779—1864), who, amongst other economic
work, edited Ricardo's writings [1] and the *Wealth of Nations*,
reproduced the same theories. NASSAU WILLIAM SENIOR [2]
(1790—1864) was indeed in many respects an exponent
of independent and original thought; but it is not until
in 1848 we reach the *Principles of Political Economy* of
JOHN STUART MILL that we can discover any distinct in-
fringement of Ricardo's supremacy, and Mill himself spoke
of the older economist with the "piety of a disciple,"
although he supplemented and amended his reasoning in
more than one important respect.

The characteristic feature of that reasoning was its
exclusively abstract nature. Ricardo assumed the prevalence of competition; and he endeavoured to ascertain
what would be, on this assumption, the natural order of the
distribution of wealth among the various classes of society.
"Political Economy," he writes in a letter to Malthus,
"you think is an enquiry into the nature and causes of
wealth; I think it should rather be called an enquiry into
the laws which determine the division of the produce of
industry amongst the classes who concur in its formation."
"Everyday I am more satisfied that the former enquiry is
vain and delusive, and the latter only the true object of
the science." His assumption of competition was, as we

---

[1] He thought it unnecessary to include among these Ricardo's "vindication of his own doctrines from the objections" of Malthus.

[2] Senior wrote a general treatise, and was perhaps the real author of
the 'wages fund theory' (see below p. 190).

F

have seen, scarcely untrue to the actual circumstances of the times; but his abstract method, of inquiry may be traced to the influence of his nationality and training.

He was born in 1772 of Jewish parentage, and he had the fondness of his race for abstract speculation. He received a commercial education, and, at the early age of fourteen, commenced his acquaintance with the Stock Exchange, of which his father was a member. When he was twenty-one years old he began business on his own account, and acquired a fortune which enabled him to retire at an early age. The sphere of activity in which he thus passed the business period of his life was calculated to increase his fondness and capacity for abstractions. As Bagehot has observed,[1] "there is no place where the calculations are so fine, or where they are employed on *data* so impalpable and so little 'immersed in matter.'" "The Jews excel on every Bourse in Europe." His association with the Stock Exchange also led him to write his first economic production on a branch of the subject where a power of abstraction was especially appropriate. This was the topic of money in its connection with foreign trade; and later economic inquiry has never failed to recognise the propriety and advantage of an abstract method in elucidating the subtle and perplexing intricacies of this topic. It is when we come to deal with the industrial relations of men to one another, and the human services remunerated by profits and wages, that an abstract method is liable to mislead, if it is not supplemented and qualified by constant reference to facts. But the work of the economists of Ricardo's time on money and foreign trade has, even in our own days, met with ungrudging approval rather than

---

[1] *Economic Studies*, p, 151.

disparaging or emending criticism. Ricardo's tract entitled *The High Price of Bullion a Proof of the Depreciation of Bank Notes* was published in 1809, and the opinions which he advocated were afterwards adopted in the Report of the Bullion Committee. In 1811 he wrote a reply to Mr. Bosanquet's *Practical Observations* on that report; in 1815 an *Essay on the Influence of a Low Price of Corn on the Profits of Stock*, in which he opposed Protection; in 1816 a pamphlet containing *Proposals for an Economical and Secure Currency*; and in 1817 *The Principles of Political Economy and Taxation.* This was his most important systematic work, but in 1820 he contributed an article on the *Funding System* to the supplement to the *Encyclopædia Britannica*, and in 1822 he published a tract on *Protection to Agriculture.* In 1819 he entered Parliament, where his influence, derived from the repute of his economic writings, seems to have been considerable. He was a zealous and outspoken advocate of Parliamentary Reform. In 1823 he died, in the fifty-second year of his age.

He seems himself to have been aware of the abstract character of his writing, and of his own deficiencies as a writer. In judging his *Principles* we have to remember that he was only induced by the pressure of friends to publish a systematic treatise, and that the treatise is so far from being systematic that it has rather the appearance of a collection of detached notes. His abstractions were also so much related to practice that the political proposals which he supported were measures of practical usefulness, and were yet based upon his economic principles. But his method was certainly very abstract; and he does not appear to have been, in the true sense of the words, a systematic writer. He is not careful to make the assumptions on which his reasoning rests clear at each successive stage in the argument. He is generally content to state them once, and then to take them for granted. A recent writer[1] has said that "he never explains himself." "My speaking," he declares himself in a letter to Malthus, "is like my writing, too much compressed. I am too apt to crowd a great deal of difficult matter into so short a space as to be incomprehensible to the generality of readers." "I am fully aware," he writes on another occasion, referring to a manuscript which he had sent, "of the deficiency in the style and arrangement: those are faults which I shall never conquer." And again: "I am but a poor master of language, and therefore I shall fail to express what I mean."

But he was careful also to emphasise the intentional nature of the abstract character of his work. Thus he writes to Malthus, "Our differences may in some respects, I think, be ascribed to your considering my book as more practical than I intended it to be. My object was to elucidate principles, and to do this I imagined strong cases, that I might show the operation of those principles." And again: "You have always in your mind the immediate and temporary effects of particular changes, whereas I put these immediate and temporary effects quite aside, and fix my whole attention on the permanent state of things which will result from them. Perhaps you estimate these temporary effects too highly, while I am too much disposed to undervalue them."

Many, and perhaps most, of the accusations, which have been freely brought against him in our days, may be traced to a misunderstanding of his own language, and this misunderstanding is often due to those deficiencies in composi-

---

[1] Professor Marshall in his *Principles of Economics*, p. 60.

tion of which he was himself conscious. Other charges are
based on the perversions of his words by other writers, but
these perversions, again, are frequently due to his own failure
to state explicitly, and repeatedly, what he takes for granted.
It is a striking illustration of the irony of fate that the
writings of so strong an individualist should have supplied
the two fundamental doctrines on which the superstructure
of modern socialism rests. And yet it is his theory of rent,
and his theory of value, which have been used to furnish a
'scientific' basis for the 'nationalisation' of land and of capital.

Ricardo put forward a theory of value, according to
which the "value of a commodity" depended "on the relative
quantity of labour which" was "necessary for its production"; and he held that the value of labour itself, or the
rate of wages, similarly depended on the cost of production
of labour, or, in other words, on the cost of the labourer's
subsistence. This theory has been used to justify the
contention of Karl Marx that the value of commodities is
due solely to the labour of the workman, and not also to
the machinery or other capital employed, that the wages of
the workman are equal to what is required for his subsistence, and that, so far as the value of the commodities
produced exceeds this amount, the surplus is appropriated
by the employer, who thus robs the workman and 'exploits'
his labour, because he has the advantage of possessing the
means of production, and can compel him to work for longer
hours than would suffice to produce enough to exchange for
the necessaries of his subsistence.

This theory of *surplus value*, which is used to support the
proposal for the collective ownership of the means of production by the State as the representative of society, bears
some resemblance to Ricardo's theory ; but the resemblance

is obtained by ignoring important differences. Ricardo qualifies his statement in several ways. He applies his theory to "such commodities only as can be increased in quantity by the exertion of human industry, and on the production of which competition operates without restraint." " In speaking " " of the exchangeable value of commodities, or the power of purchasing possessed by any one commodity," he means "always that power which it would possess, if not disturbed by any temporary or accidental cause." He allows that "the principle that the quantity of labour bestowed on the production of commodities regulates their relative value " is " considerably modified by the employment of machinery and other fixed and durable capital. He maintains that the "natural price of labour depends " " on the quantity of food," necessaries and conveniences become essential " to the labourer "from habit," and that the " market rate " of wages "may, in an improving society, for an indefinite period, be constantly above " this "natural rate," which itself " varies at different times in the same country, and very materially differs in different countries." All these qualifications are made by Ricardo himself, and it is only by ignoring their general drift that the theory of surplus value can be regarded as the logical outcome of his reasoning.

To his theory of rent we may devote more detailed attention. It is that part of his work by which he is perhaps best known. It is true that he can be called the author of the theory with less accuracy than Malthus can be considered responsible for the doctrine of population. Not only Malthus himself in his *Inquiry into the Nature and Progress of Rent*, which was published in 1815, but Sir EDWARD WEST also, in an anonymous *Essay on the Application of Capital to Land*, written under the name of "a

Fellow of University College, Oxford," had, as Ricardo states himself in his preface, "presented to the world, nearly at the same moment, the true doctrine of rent"; and, so far back as 1777, DR. ANDERSON seems to have stated the theory in his *Enquiry into the Nature of the Corn Laws.* But its connection with the name of Ricardo in the history of Political Economy is not without justification. His treatment has been generally adopted, and he founded his whole economic doctrine upon it. "Without a knowledge" of it, he writes, "it is impossible to understand the effect of the progress of wealth on profits and wages, or to trace satisfactorily the influence of taxation on different classes of the community."

In the second chapter of his *Principles*, accordingly, immediately after the exposition of value which is contained in the first, he deals with rent. "Rent" he defines as "that portion of the produce of the earth which is paid to the landlord for the use of the original and indestructible powers of the soil." This is the "strict sense" of the term, and must be distinguished from that "popular sense," which is found in Adam Smith, and, applying the term to "whatever is annually paid by a farmer to his landlord," confounds "the interest and profit of capital" with it.

Having framed his definition of rent, Ricardo proceeds to consider how it arises. "On the first settling of a country," he writes, "in which there is an abundance of rich and fertile land, a very small proportion of which is required to be cultivated for the support of the actual population," "there will be no rent; for no one would pay for the use of land, when there was an abundant quantity not yet appropriated, and, therefore, at the disposal of whosoever might choose to cultivate it." "On the common principles of supply and demand, no rent could be paid for such land." "If," indeed, "all land had the same properties, if it were unlimited in quantity, and uniform in quality, no charge could be made for its use, unless where it possessed peculiar advantages of situation. It is only, then, because land is not unlimited in quantity and uniform in quality, and because, in the progress of population, land of an inferior quality, or less advantageously situated, is called into cultivation, that rent is ever paid for the use of it. When, in the progress of society, land of the second degree of fertility is taken into cultivation, rent immediately commences on that of the first quality, and the amount of that rent will depend on the difference in the quality of these two portions of land. When land of the third quality is taken into cultivation, rent immediately commences on the second, and it is regulated as before, by the difference in their productive powers. At the same time, the rent of the first quality will rise, for that must always be above the rent of the second, by the difference between the produce which they yield with a given quantity of capital and labour. "It often" "and indeed commonly happens," however, "that before" "the inferior lands are cultivated, capital can be employed more productively on those lands which are already in cultivation," but with a "diminished return." "In such case, capital will be preferably employed on the old land, and will equally create a rent; for rent is always the difference between the produce obtained by the employment of two equal quantities of capital and labour."

But what is the reason of this? It is that the "exchangeable value of all commodities," and, amongst these, of "the produce of land," "is always regulated, not by the less quantity of labour that will suffice for their production

under circumstances highly favourable, and exclusively enjoyed by those who have peculiar facilities of production;
but by the greater quantity of labour necessarily bestowed
on their production by those who have no such facilities;
by those who contrive to produce them under the most
unfavourable circumstances; meaning, by the most unfavourable circumstances, the most unfavourable under which the
quantity of produce required renders it necessary to carry
on the production." "When land of an inferior quality is
taken into cultivation, the exchangeable value of raw produce
will rise, because more labour is required to produce it."
"It is true, that on the best land, the same produce would
still be obtained with the same labour as before, but its
value would be enhanced;" and the "advantages" thus
resulting are "transferred from the cultivator, or consumer,
to the landlord."

This, then, is the way in which rent arises. We start with
the market, and we find that the price of "the produce of
land" is regulated by that part of the supply, which is produced, and brought to market, at the greatest expense. The
price obtained by this must be sufficient to repay the expense
of producing it, and bringing it to market, and to yield the
"usual and general rate of profits on stock;" or it will not
come. But the price will not rise above this point, and will
yield no rent, while those who produce at greater advantages,
obtaining the same price for that which has cost less to
produce, have a surplus in hand, which competition compels
them to transfer to the landlord as rent.

It may be observed that Ricardo's statement affords an
illustration of that lack of systematic expression and ordered
arrangement which was previously noted. He defines [1] rent

---

[1] This is an alternative definition to that quoted above.

as "that compensation which is paid to the owner of land
for the use of its original and indestructible powers," and
apparently all that he has in his mind at the moment is the
"natural fertility of the soil." But, before he has gone very
far in his exposition, it seems to occur to him that "advantages of situation" have also an importance of their
own, although it is straining language to reckon them, as
apparently he does, as part of "the original and indestructible
powers of the soil." They may be due to extraneous improvements in the means of communication with the market.
However, he now introduces this fresh element of "advantages of situation," but the introduction is effected by
a qualifying clause, which has the appearance of being
incidental; and, after proceeding to trace the rise of rent
by differences of fertility alone, it is only at the end that he
becomes more comprehensive, and says that the "exchangeable value" of the "produce" of "the most fertile and favourably situated land" "will be adjusted by the total quantity
of labour necessary in various forms, from first to last, to
produce it and bring it to market." It is this lack of strict
systematic expression which later economists have endeavoured to supply, and, had his own statement been
more explicit, he would probably have avoided considerable
misunderstanding. In a similar way there are, according to
his statement, three causes of rent; but they are not distinctly set forth, or arranged together. One is the difference of natural fertility between different soils, the second,
the difference of situation with reference to the market,
and the third, the difference in the returns to capital and
labour on the same soil, owing to the action of the law of
diminishing returns.

From his theory of rent he draws certain conclusions.

The first is that "corn is not high because a rent is paid, but a rent is paid because corn is high; and it has been justly observed that no reduction would take place in the price of corn, although landlords should forego the whole of their rent."

The second is that writers like Adam Smith were wrong in supposing that rent was a mark of "the advantages which the land possesses over every other source of useful produce," and a sign that in agriculture "nature labours along with man." "There is not a manufacture," Ricardo writes, "in which nature does not give assistance to man;" and he quotes with approval the commentary made by Buchanan [1] on Adam Smith's words. "It is not from the produce, but from the price at which the produce is sold, that rent is derived; and this price is got not because nature assists in the production, but because it is the price which suits the consumption to the supply." "When land is most abundant," Ricardo observes, "when most productive, and most fertile, it yields no rent; and it is only when its powers decay, and less is yielded in return for labour, that a share of the original produce of the more fertile portions is set apart for rent." "The rise of rent" may be a "symptom, but it is never a cause of wealth." It may be a "symptom," for it is always the "effect" of increasing wealth, and of "the "difficulty of providing food for" an "augmented population"; and "population" itself "increases or diminishes with the increase or diminution of capital." But, on the other hand, "wealth often increases most rapidly while rent is either stationary, or even falling;" for this increase takes place "where the disposable land is most fertile, where importation is least restricted, and where, through agricultural

---

[1] David Buchanan edited the *Wealth of Nations* in 1814.

improvements, productions can be multiplied without any increase in the proportional quantity of labour, and where consequently the progress of rent is slow." "The wealth and population of a country" may be increased, and yet, if that increase is "accompanied" by "marked improvements in agriculture," rent may be lowered. Such improvements are of two kinds. They may "increase the productive powers of the land" by the "more skilful rotation of crops, or the better choice of manure." Or they may "enable us, by improving our machinery, to obtain" the "produce of land with less labour. "Improvements in agricultural implements, such as the plough and thrashing machine, economy in the use of horses employed in husbandry, and a better knowledge of the veterinary art, are of this nature." The "immediate effect" of both kinds of improvements is to "lower rent," although they may be "ultimately of immense advantage to landlords," by giving a "great stimulus to population."

Thirdly, and lastly, it is on his theory of rent that Ricardo bases his conception of the 'natural' order of the distribution of wealth, and of the future condition of society. His theory of wages and his theory of profits are intimately related to his theory of rent, and his theory of the incidence of the various forms of taxation rests on the same basis. Wages depend on the "price of the food, necessaries and conveniences required for the support of the labourer and his family"; and, "with a rise in the price of food and necessaries, the natural price of labour will rise," as it will fall "with the fall in their price." Profits in their turn "depend on wages," for "the whole value" of the "commodities" of the "farmer" and the "manufacturer" "is divided into two portions only," one of which "constitutes the profits of stock, the other the wages of labour." "Neither the farmer who cultivates that

quantity of land, which regulates price, nor the manufacturer
who manufactures goods, sacrifice any portion of the produce
for rent." And so the general position is reached, "Profits
depend on high or low wages, wages on the prices of
necessaries, and the price of necessaries chiefly on the
price of food, because all other requisites may be increased
almost without limit," for the simple reason that the "rise
in the natural price of the raw material," of which such
requisites are made, is "more than counterbalanced by the
improvements in machinery, by the better division and
distribution of labour, and by the increasing skill, both in
science and art, of the producers." Or, as the position is
differently and more briefly stated in another passage, "In
all countries, and all times, profits depend on the quantity
of labour requisite to provide necessaries for the labourers
on that land, or with that capital which yields no rent."

From this general position a conclusion follows respecting
the future of society: "In the progress of society and wealth,
the additional quantity of food requisite is obtained by the
sacrifice of more and more labour." The "natural tendency,"
therefore, of wages is to rise in money value, in order to
purchase the requisite food, but to remain constant, or
to slightly fall, in their real value, or command over the
necessaries of subsistence, as the pressure of population on
the resources of land increases. The "natural tendency" of
profits is to fall in consequence of the diminishing pro-
ductiveness of land, and the constant, or slightly diminished,
requirements of subsistence of labour, although the tendency
may for a time be arrested by "improvements in agriculture,"
or the "discovery of new markets, whence provisions may
be imported." The "natural tendency" of rent is to increase,
if not immediately, at least in the long run.

These are the main points of Ricardo's position as it is expounded in his *Principles of Political Economy and Taxation*, and also in his earlier *Essay on the Influence of a Low Price of Corn on the Profits of Stock*, and his later pamphlet on *Protection to Agriculture*. Professor SIDGWICK has said [1] that what is known as the Ricardian theory of rent "combines, in a somewhat confusing way, at least three distinct theories," of which the first is a "historical theory as to the origin of rent," the second a "statical theory of the economic forces tending to determine rent at the present time," and the third a "dynamical theory of the causes continually tending to increase rent, as wealth and population increases."

The theory has been subjected to severe criticism from various standpoints. The American economist Carey has urged that the historical order of cultivation assumed by Ricardo is incorrect. It is not always the case, and actual American experience has afforded an illustration, that the richer soils are taken first into cultivation, and that in the progress of society cultivation extends downwards to the poorer land. There may be circumstances, such as the necessity of defence from hostile attack, or the expenditure requisite to bring certain land under cultivation, which lead men in an early stage of civilisation to occupy the poorer hillsides in preference to the richer valleys; and then, in the progress of society, when the advantage of a position secured against the assaults of enemies becomes less urgent, and the initial expenditure of draining, it may be, or fencing, is more easily met, the soils which are naturally richer are brought under cultivation, and substituted for those which are naturally poorer.

[1] *Principles of Political Economy*, Bk. II , ch. vii., sec. 1.

This criticism is instructive, but it does not seem to be conclusive. The Ricardian theory, when liberally interpreted, affirms that men bring under cultivation in the first instance those soils which they consider at the time to possess the greatest advantages, and that cultivation extends afterwards under the pressure of population to less advantageous soils. The advantage may consist in natural fertility, or it may consist in situation, or possibly in other circumstances, and the total advantage can only be determined when we take into account all these factors, of which one may outweigh or be neutralised by another. What the criticism seems especially to show is that the conception of a constant tendency to an increase in rent, which Ricardo had formed, needs considerable qualification. For the progress of society may not only change the situation of different soils with reference to the market where the produce is sold, by altering the routes, or improving the means of communication and transport, but it may also affect their natural fertility, by substituting one method of cultivation or variety of crop for another. It may lessen and not increase the differences between the advantages of different soils, and it may postpone the diminution in the average return to capital.

It is only by a liberal interpretation that the Ricardian theory can be considered adequate, whether we regard it as an explanation of the past, or a statement of the present, or a prediction of the future. The theory maintains that, viewed from the stand-point of the present, rent is equivalent to the differences between the returns yielded to the application of capital (and labour) to land under the most disadvantageous circumstances, and the returns yielded to their application under more advantageous conditions. As a statement of the present, this conclusion seems to be a necessary corollary from the market price of the produce of land; for that is determined by the expense of production of that part which is produced at the greatest expense, and other producers, realising the same price, and finding their expenses less, have a differential advantage, which competition for the enjoyment of their position compels them to transfer to the landlords as rent.

The theory is based on the assumption of competition; and, so far as competition is hindered in its action, it fails to accord with fact. It assumes that landlord and tenant respectively are actuated by competitive considerations alone; that the landlord endeavours to obtain the highest rent he can, and the tenant the lowest; that both are independent, intelligent agents, able and willing to carry their wares and services to the best market; that the landlord will not be influenced by kindly feeling, or political obligation, or long connection; and that the tenant produces with a single view to the sale of his produce, and, knowing all the advantages of different soils, and places, and trades, is able and willing to move, taking with him his improvements or their value, to any soil, or place, or trade, where he will be more favourably situated.

This assumption, however, is seldom completely realised. The system of landlord and tenant is far from being the universal form of tenure; and the influence of custom modifies the action and effects of competition. The peasant proprietor does not cultivate with a single eye to the sale of the entire produce of his land, but he and his family consume part of that produce; and he can only be said to pay a rent to himself, for he is at once landlord, farmer, and labourer. The metayer, again, who is found in districts of Southern Europe, pays a rent, it is true, to a landlord, who furnishes, according to the custom of the district, a varying part of the capital needed for cultivating the land ; but the rent is a definite proportion of the produce determined by custom, and not by competition.   The Indian ryot, or zemindar, pays his rent in the form of a land-tax to the Government ; but this again is fixed for a long period, or in perpetuity, and is regulated to a great extent by custom.   Nor does the English landlord exact in every case an extreme com-petitive rent for the use of his land, and dismiss at once the tenant who will not pay it ; while the Irish cottier had practically no other occupation into which he could turn his energies but that of cultivating land, and could not, therefore, compare his earnings with those obtained in other employments.   In the first of these two last cases rents are probably on the whole below, in the other they were apparently above, the level which would be fixed by active independent competition on both sides of the contract. In all these instances the assumption of competition is very useful as a basis of inquiry; but it is liable to considerable modification when it is applied to the explanation of actual fact.

But the theory has been criticised on other grounds. It has been said that it is not possible to discover any land which yields 'no rent,' but only the expenses of production and ordinary farming profits.   To this the reply has been made that, although a farm as a whole may thus pay rent, the differences in quality of its various portions may be such that part may be considered to contribute nothing in that form.   Ricardo himself met the objection by urging that the theory would be equally valid, if there were an application of capital to land which yielded 'no rent.'   The last, or marginal, *'dose'* of capital applied—to use James Mill's suggestive phrase—yields no more than the expenses of production and ordinary farming profits, and the previous 'doses,' or the 'doses' applied under more favourable circumstances, yield in comparison a surplus. It may be urged also that, even if there were not any 'no-rent' land, or 'no-rent' application of capital to land, yet the rent yielded in some cases might be so small that in comparison it might be properly treated as *nil;* and that, in any event, differences in relative advantage would exist.

These difficulties have recently presented themselves in another form. The theory is based on the relative advantages of different applications of capital to land measured upwards from a minimum level where 'no rent,' or next to none, is paid.   But it is possible that these advantages may vary at the same or different times, according as the rates of wages and profits vary, and according as land is sown with different crops, or cultivated by different methods, or its produce is sent to different markets by different routes or means of communication.   The land, which is a 'no-rent,' or inferior, land with reference to one crop, may not be so with regard to another, and similar considerations apply to the case of different rates of profits and wages, and different markets and methods of cultivation and transport.   Such considerations as these are important ; and they undoubtedly affect also the validity of Ricardo's conception of the causes continually tending to increase rent in the future.

This conception has been recently used to support the socialistic scheme of the 'nationalisation of land.'   Rent, in the economic sense of the term, it has been urged, is due to the ' inherent qualities' of the soil—to its natural fertility, or its situation with regard to the market; and it is con-

tinually increasing in amount, as population and wealth
increase. Why then should not society, or the State as
its representative, appropriate for the common benefit this
growing fund, which is due to nature or society at large
rather than to individual landlords, and tends at present to
the advantage of one class of the community at the expense
of others? This is the conception of the 'unearned increment'; and it is based on the Ricardian theory of rent.

But it is difficult to apply the nice distinctions of that
theory to practical affairs. The changing methods of
cultivation, and communication with the market, may convert
what is at one time an 'unearned increment' into an 'unearned decrement' at another; and of recent years the
cultivation of virgin soils in America, and the decrease
in the cost of transporting foreign grain, have occasioned
a serious fall in agricultural rents in old countries like
England, and robbed them to a certain extent of the
'natural protection' they may have derived from their
proximity to the market, or the quality of their land.

Ricardo was aware that this would be, for the time at
least, the result of the "discovery of new markets whence
provisions" could "be imported," and of "improvements" in
agricultural science and practice. But he formed a restricted
idea of the extent of these changes; for, like Malthus, he
was no 'geographer,' and the law of diminishing returns
seemed to be rigorously applying to English agriculture.
Nor did he sufficiently recognise the benefits of a dense
population in permitting division and organisation of
labour, and, by an increase in the product of industry,
allowing of an advance in wages and profits, of the determination of which he seems to have formed too rigid
and absolute a conception. Nor, again, did he take into

consideration the question of such an application of land
to different crops, or uses, that the returns, which were
diminishing under the old, might increase under the new
application, and the relative advantages of different soils
be altered.

Another serious difficulty confronts the proposal to apply
to practice the theoretical conception of the 'unearned
increment.' How can economic 'rent,' strictly so called,
be distinguished from interest or profits? How can the
'no-rent' land which only yields profits, or the 'no-rent'
application of capital to land, be identified? How far is
the produce of land due to its "original and indestructible
powers," and how far to the expenditure and labour of
landlords and tenants? How far is the 'increment,' or
'decrement,' as the case may be, 'earned' or 'unearned'?
"In popular language," as Ricardo allows, the term "rent"
"is applied to whatever is annually paid by a farmer to his
landlord"; and, although in his chapter on Rent he is
"desirous of confining" the term to its "strict sense," in a
foot-note to his eighteenth chapter on the Poor Rates he
says that "part" of the capital applied to the "improvement" of land, "when once expended," "is inseparably
amalgamated with the land, and tends to increase its
productive powers," and that "the remuneration paid to the
landlord for its use is strictly of the nature of rent, and is
subject to all the laws of rent." But, although regarded from
the stand-point of the present it is a differential advantage
in favour of the land in question, and is indistinguishable
from "its original and indestructible powers," viewed from
a historical stand-point, it is 'earned' and not 'unearned.'
Carey, indeed, and others, have pushed this historical argument so far as to contend that rent represents nothing more

than a return for what has been expended on the cultivation of land in the past; and, although their contention is open to criticism on the ground that some of the outlay on agricultural improvements is expended once for all, and does not recur, and is undertaken with the expectation that the return will suffice, not only to pay the interest, but also to repay the principal, within a limited time, there is no doubt, as Ricardo himself says, that the improvement "will not be undertaken in the first instance, unless there is a strong probability that the return will at least be equal to the profit that can be made by the disposition of any other equal capital."

The difficulty of distinguishing that part of 'rent' which is 'earned' from that which is 'unearned' is a crucial difficulty. There may be instances of agricultural land, where the distinction can be more readily established; and it can be drawn with greater ease in the case of urban land, where we find differences of 'economic rent' due to the suitability of different sites for various employments, and to their relative situation, and also differences of rent, in the popular use of the term, due to the expenditure of landlords or tenants in the bricks and mortar of a house, or the improvement of the ground.

But in many, and perhaps most, cases the difficulty of drawing the distinction is very great, and in not a few it seems insuperable. The way in which the conception of an 'unearned increment' has been extended to other forms of wealth besides land, like the possession of fine pictures, or extraordinary business or professional opportunities, illustrates the difficulty. On the one hand the incomes thus derived may be due in some degree, like rent, to causes apart from the action of their possessors, and on the other it seems impossible to say how far they are, and how far they are not, thus due.   The case is less obscure with regard to land, but it is not clear.   As an explanation, therefore, of the action and results of free competition in connection with land, Ricardo's theory helps to disentangle what would otherwise be very intricate; but, in its application to practical affairs, it requires great discrimination.   The intellectual discipline necessary for a thorough and accurate grasp of its theoretic bearings might well beget a wise caution in practice; and Ricardo is not alone, or entirely, responsible for the misunderstanding, or misapplication, of his views by unpractical or untheoretical followers.

CHAPTER IV.

JOHN STUART MILL. 1806—1873.

THE THEORY OF VALUE.

THERE are few, if there are any, writers who have exercised
a more profound or extensive influence over the general
thought and opinion of Englishmen during the last half-
century or so than JOHN STUART MILL. Nor is it difficult
to account for this ; for he wrote on a variety of subjects,
and, amongst them, on some which concern the highest and

most permanent interests of men. The education, which was imparted to him by his father, and described by himself in his *Autobiography*, has not yet ceased to excite astonishment. He characterises it as "unusual" and "remarkable." His earliest recollections carried him back to the days when, a child of some three years of age, he committed to memory lists of Greek words written by his father on cards. From three to seven he was occupied with Greek, history, and arithmetic; and the list of books he read is long and varied. At seven years of age he began Latin, and, about twelve, logic, and, a little later, political economy. He then, in 1820, went for a year to France, and continued the same routine of incessant study. Nor did his studies end with his return to England, for, he writes, "my education resumed its ordinary course." "I continued my old studies, with the addition of some new ones." He worked for some nine hours a day, and there can be little doubt that he overtaxed his strength in these early years. Of course he may not, and we may almost say that he could not, have entirely assimilated this vast mass of material; but it undoubtedly contributed to increase the variety of the topics on which he afterwards wrote, and to produce the breadth of knowledge with which he handled them.

Among these many subjects of study there were some on which his early attainments were most remarkable, and his later performances promise perhaps to be most enduring. These were Logic, Politics, and Political Economy. His father was himself most interested in these subjects, and laid the greatest stress upon them. James Mill, who is sometimes distinguished as the 'elder Mill,' was unquestionably a remarkable figure of the time in which he lived. He exercised an extraordinary personal influence over his con temporaries ; and he is even said to have resembled Socrates in his power of making those who conversed with him sift their ideas, and aim at pure unadulterated truth.   It was his habit to take his son for walks, and discuss the subjects which he was studying.   The boy made notes on slips of paper of his reading as he went on, and with their assistance he had to give an account of it during these walks.   From the very first he was compelled to think for himself, and his father would never explain a difficulty to him until he had fully realised it, and made a serious effort to solve it. The education, wide as the ground was which it covered, was not mere 'cram,' but it was intellectually stimulating in a high degree.

The occupation of his later life afforded him leisure for abundant literary work.   In 1823, when he was seventeen years of age, he obtained a post in the India House, immediately under his father, and he was finally appointed Examiner of Indian Correspondence in 1856, two years previous to the transference of the government of India to the Crown, and his own retirement.   He said himself that there could be no employment more suitable for literary pursuits, and he found his "office duties an actual rest" from his "other mental occupations."   They had the additional advantage of making him realise practical difficulties, and of compelling him to habitually put his thoughts into a shape which could be readily understood.   To this habit we may attribute in some measure the characteristic lucidity of his writings, and his faculty of giving easy expression to abstract argument.

For a time, indeed, after his retirement from the India House, he discharged parliamentary duties, exchanging, as he himself said, his "tranquil and retired existence as a

writer of books," "for the less congenial occupation of a
member of the House of Commons." Mr. Gladstone has
recently stated[1] that, during his presence in Parliament, he
was sensible of a "singular moral elevation" about him;
but that presence was comparatively brief, and he was the
successful candidate for Westminster at the election of 1865,
only to be defeated three years later. He died at Avignon
in 1873.

The diversity of his early reading may have had a further
consequence beyond those we have noted. At any rate he
was singularly fair-minded. He was conscientiously anxious
to do justice to an opponent, and to state that opponent's
view in the fairest way, even though he were himself opposed
to it, and intended to rebut it. He was ever "ready," in
his own words, to "learn and unlearn"; and he showed
this in his economic studies by the frankness and completeness with which he abandoned in later life the theory of a
fixed 'wage-fund,'[2] on which he had previously insisted. At
one period of his early life it was his custom to meet twice
a week with other young men, and discuss the books they
had read; and he himself attributes to these conversations
his "real inauguration as an original and independent
thinker." His father, moreover, had carefully guarded
against encouraging any idea of self-conceit, and had
endeavoured to make him feel how little he really knew.

But, were we to stop here, we should have given an
inadequate account of his intellectual characteristics. The
most important chapter of his *Autobiography* is that in
which he describes the change that passed over him at what
he terms a "crisis" in his "mental history." He had been

[1] In a letter printed in Mr. W. L. Courtney's *Mill.*
[2] See below, pp. 190-2.

brought up by his father in the strictest tenets of a very strict
school. The school of thought in which he was trained
discountenanced feeling and imagination as mere senti-
ment, and regarded rigid thought and severe analytical
reasoning as alone desirable. It was the school of JEREMY
BENTHAM,[1] and it held that the complex phenomena of
society could be explained in the light of a few simple
principles. It believed implicitly in representative government. It maintained that the goal of all legislative effort
should be the "greatest happiness of the greatest number,"
and that the surest road by which to travel to reach this
end was that of reducing governmental interference to the
minimum, and of affording to the individual the maximum
of liberty of action and discussion. It declared that the
source of all morality was an 'enlightened selfishness,' each
man pursuing that course of action which would bring him
the greatest pleasure or the least pain, and that the interests
of the individual coincided with the interests of the community. It contended that our minds were but "bundles
of sensations," and our characters the result of the moulding
of circumstance. It thought that jurisprudence could be explained by the rigid analysis of a few such terms as sove-
reignty, right and duty, psychology by the principle of the
"association of ideas," ethics by that of the "greatest happiness of the greatest number," and economics by that of
laissez-faire and the doctrine of population. "Euclid
was to this school," as Bagehot has graphically put it,[2] "the
one type of scientific thought."

In his *Autobiography* Mill describes how, after reading

---

[1] Bentham himself wrote upon economics, notably in his *Defence of
Usury* (1787).

[2] *Economic Studies*, p. 156.

Bentham in a French reproduction, the "feeling rushed
upon" him "that all previous moralists were superseded,
and that here indeed was the commencement of a new era
in thought." Here was "intellectual clearness," and here
were also "the most inspiring prospects of practical improvement in human affairs." "Now," he writes, he "had
opinions; a creed, a doctrine, a philosophy; in one among
the best senses of the word, a religion; the inculcation and
diffusion of which could be made the principal outward
purpose of a life." And inculcate and diffuse it accordingly
he did. A little society, called the "Utilitarian Society"
was formed in the winter of 1822-23, and consisted of young
men, "acknowledging Utility as their standard in ethics and
politics," and meeting once a fortnight for the reading of
essays, and the discussion of questions. The new *Westminster
Review* was the organ of publication to a larger world of
those doctrines of utility and other kindred principles, which
were afterwards known as ' Philosophical Radicalism.'

But a change came. In the autumn of 1826 he
awakened from his "dream." It "occurred" to him "to
put the question directly" to himself: "'Suppose that all
your objects in life were realised; that all the changes in
institutions and opinions which you are looking forward to,
could be completely effected at this very instant: would
this be a great joy and happiness to you?'" "And an
irrepressible self-consciousness distinctly answered, 'No.'"
At this his "heart sank within" him, and "the whole
foundation on which" his "life was constructed fell down."

"At first" he "hoped that the cloud would pass away of
itself; but it did not." On the contrary it "seemed to grow
thicker and thicker." "In vain" he "sought relief from" his
"favourite books": they could not help him. Nor could he

find assistance in his father's advice; for his education,
which had been "wholly" his father's work, "had been
conducted without any regard to the possibility of its ending
in this result." The "habit of analysis," which had been the
centre of his father's system, had a "tendency to wear away
the feelings," and needed "complements and correctives."
"The pleasure of sympathy with human beings, and the
feelings which made the good of others, and especially of
mankind on a large scale, the object of existence" might be,
and probably were, the "greatest and surest sources of
happiness." But the knowledge that they were so, which
might be disclosed by analysis, did not impart the feelings;
and Mill considered rather that he "was left stranded at the
commencement of" his "voyage, with a well-equipped ship,
and a rudder, but no sail," no "real desire for the ends" he
"had been so carefully fitted out to work for, no delight in
virtue, or the general good, but also just as little in anything
else."

After half a year of this feeling, a "small ray of light broke
in upon" his "gloom." He was reading, by accident,
Marmontel's *Mémoires*, and he "came to the passage which
relates his father's death, the distressed position of the
family, and the sudden inspiration by which he, then a mere
boy, felt and made them feel that he would be everything
to them—would supply the place of all that they had lost."
Reading this account, Mill was "moved to tears"; and
from that moment his "burden grew lighter." He knew
that he had "feeling," and that he "was not a stock or a
stone." And now his "theory of life" was altered. He now
felt that, although "happiness" might indeed be the "test of
all rules of conduct, and the end of life," it "was only to be
attained by not making it the direct end." "Those only"

were "happy, who" had "their minds fixed on some object
other than their own happiness; on the happiness of others,
on the improvement of mankind, even on some art or
pursuit, followed not as a means, but as itself an ideal end."
From that time, too, forward, he gave a place "among the
prime necessities of human well-being, to the internal
culture of the individual," and "ceased to attach almost
exclusive importance to the ordering of outward circumstances, and the training of the human being for speculation and for action." He began to cultivate his feelings,
he strengthened the interest he already felt in music, and
he took a fresh interest in the poetry of Wordsworth.

The fact was that he had a warm, sympathetic, and
emotional side to his nature, and that he now burst asunder
the bonds in which his father's stern and rigid system had
confined him. The influence of this emancipation made
itself felt in all the various departments of his intellectual
activity, and tended to produce those inconsistencies, apparent
or real, which have been discovered in his writings by the
scrutiny of unfriendly critics. The recoil from the narrow
creed of his earlier years gave place after a time to a
reaction from that recoil, and he endeavoured to re-
concile the new faith he had gained with the old, and to
combine the more tender and human doctrine with that
which was more severe and more rigidly abstract.

He may not have been always successful in the attempt.
He introduces elements into his philosophy which some
critics have held to be really destructive of the basis on
which it is ostensibly founded. The theory that character
is due to the moulding of outward circumstances is qualified
by the reflection put forward in his *Logic*, which was published
in 1843, that we may ourselves help to shape those circum-

stances. The theory that the morality of actions is tested by the amount of pleasure or pain that results is modified by the conception introduced into his *Essay on Utilitarianism*, which was published in 1863, that there may be differences of quality as well as of quantity in pleasures, and that some may be higher than others. And similarly, in politics and political economy, he no longer holds in an absolute form the belief that the goal of all legislative effort is to be entire liberty of action for the individual, and non-interference on the part of the government; but he now says that the "admitted functions of government embrace a much wider field than can easily be included within the ring-fence of any restrictive definition; and that it is hardly possible to find any ground of justification common to them all, except the comprehensive one of general expediency, nor to limit the interference of government by any universal rule, save the simple and vague one that it should never be admitted but when the case of expediency is strong."

Mill's economic writings, indeed, might be said to be tinged with a diluted socialism, and he states himself that he was influenced by the socialistic literature of the "St. Simonian school in France" at the time when he was passing through the "crisis in" his "mental history." In his *Principles of Political Economy* he draws a distinction, which he says he was the first to establish, between the laws of the production of wealth, which form the subject of his first book, and the laws of its distribution, which are discussed in the second. The first are "real laws of nature, dependent on the properties of objects," and cannot be modified; but the second are only the "necessary consequences of particular social arrangements," and are "liable to be much altered by the progress of social improvement."

And so he "looked forward to a time" when a social order
would prevail unlike the existing economic *régime*.   "The
social problem of the future," would, he considered, be how
to "unite the greatest individual liberty of action, with a
common ownership in the raw material of the globe, and.
an equal participation of all in the benefits of combined
labour."   This socialistic tendency seems to have been
partly due to the influence of Mrs. Taylor, who became
his wife, and he himself states that the distinction between
the laws of production and those of distribution was made
at her suggestion.   The affection, which he felt for her,
amounted to a reverence which was almost extravagant;
and it is a sure indication of the strength of the emotional
side of his nature.

   We may define his position in the history of English
political economy by saying that his work seems to mark a
transitional stage.   He was, in a sense, if we may give an
interpretation to the phrase which differs slightly from that
in which it was originally applied,[1] the *Secrétaire de la·
Rédaction*, systematising and arranging the ideas of his
predecessors in his five books on Production, Distribution,
Exchange, the Influence of the Progress of Society, and the
Influence of Government, so as to form one great whole ;
and he sometimes spoke of Ricardo "with the piety of a
disciple."   But he imported a human element into Ricardo's
abstractions ; and he stated his theories more guardedly,
and supplemented them by many qualifications.   In his
own early *Essays on some Unsettled Questions of Political
Economy*, which were published in 1844, but written in
1829 and 1830, he had formed the idea of constructing a
theoretical science which should be rigidly abstract; but

   [1] Cf. Bagehot's *Economic Studies*, p. 19.

when he published his great book in 1848 he had moved away from this conception. Its title is: *Principles of Political Economy with some of their Applications to Social Philosophy*, and he states in the preface that its "design" is "different from that of any treatise on Political Economy which has been produced in England since the work of Adam Smith." "The most characteristic quality of that work" is, he maintains, "that it invariably associates the principles with their applications," and, in these applications, Adam Smith "perpetually appeals to other and often far larger considerations than pure Political Economy affords." The note thus struck in the preface is dominant throughout, and the reforming zeal which characterises Mill's applications of his principles to social practice may be held responsible for some of his apparent or real inconsistencies, as others may be traced to the changes which he made in successive editions.

His general attitude, then, is transitional, and his treatment is wanting in finality. Critics have urged that the tendency to socialism manifested in some of his chapters is inconsistent with his strenuous support of a system of peasant proprietors in others, and they have declared that the position he takes up [1] in his fifth book "on the influence of government" is lame and halting. But his work has its conspicuous merits as well as its drawbacks. There may be some inconsistencies, and the theory may not always be fully developed, or the facts be entirely harmonious with the theory. But the inconsistencies are often more apparent than real, and the whole book is marked by a tone of moral elevation, a contagious enthusiasm for human improvement, and an inspiring belief in the possibility of accomplishing that improvement, even

---

[1] See the passage quoted above on page 95.

though it be by gradual stages. It brings an element of
humanity to bear on subjects which had sometimes received
a dry unsympathetic treatment ; and, partly in consequence
of this very element, it suggests some of the ways in which
the older doctrines may be qualified and amended.

On one point, however, with a confidence which was
unusual in him, Mill claimed to have attained finality.
This was the theory of value, which he expounded in his
third book. "Happily, there is nothing," he writes, "in
the laws of Value, which remains for the present or any
future writer to clear up; the theory of the subject is
complete; the only difficulty to be overcome is that of so
stating it as to solve by anticipation the chief perplexities
which occur in applying it." If these remarks are interpreted in a liberal sense, they may be regarded as
substantially true ; but the interpretation must needs be so
liberal as to amount to looseness. Mill's exposition of the
theory remains to this day unshaken in its fundamental bases ;
but he had stated it himself better than his predecessors had
done, and here, as elsewhere, he had supplied many of the
necessary qualifications of their doctrines. It contains some
of his best and most enduring work. But in some respects it
also illustrates the transitional nature of his work. Considerable developments of the theory have been made since he
wrote, and he never brought his theory of distribution into
harmony with it. With all his recognition of the importance
of the theory, he does not seem to have grasped the conception of it, which is now prevalent, as the central theory
of economics, applicable to the exchange of commodities,
and of services, in domestic, and international, markets.

He was, however, fully sensible of its importance, for he
states that the "question of Value is fundamental" in modern

industrial society. "The smallest error on that subject infects with corresponding error all our other conclusions; and anything vague or misty in our conception of it creates confusion and uncertainty in everything else." If, then, we desire to determine the position occupied by Mill in the history of English economics, and to gain an appreciation of the character of his work, we can hardly select for examination a better example of his method than his treatment of what he himself describes as a "fundamental" question, and other writers, before and since, have regarded as the central part, if not the whole, of political economy. That examination may be conveniently conducted by reviewing the theory as it is now presented, and discovering how much of that presentation may be found in Mill himself, and how much is due to the work of subsequent writers.

As we saw, when we were considering the work of Adam Smith,[1] the division of labour implies a market, and exchanges in that market. The question at once presents itself—on what terms will these exchanges be effected? How much must a man give of his own goods in order to obtain a certain amount of the goods of his neighbours? How much of those goods can be obtained in exchange for a certain amount of his own? Here it is that the theory of value comes in, for the value of a man's own productions, or possessions, is measured by the amount of the productions, or possessions, of other people which can be obtained in exchange for them, and the value of the productions, or possessions, of other people is measured by the amount of his own which he will give in exchange; and the economic theory of value is based on an inquiry into the conditions and circumstances which influence and determine the

[1] Page 23.

transaction.   The outline of such an inquiry is to be found in the *Wealth of Nations*, and it has recently been described as the 'chief work' of Adam Smith.   The outline was more sharply defined by Ricardo and his followers, but it was left for Mill to fill in much of the necessary shading.   As the theory left his hands it had most of the essential details of a finished drawing, and the work of succeeding writers, like Jevons and Cairnes, has mainly consisted in bringing some one of these details into greater prominence.   The most recent treatise[1] which has appeared in England may be described as an attempt to restore the due proportion to these details, and to produce a harmonious and unified presentation of the whole picture.

On both sides of the exchange, then, there are persons, and there are commodities; and from one point of view each of the persons is a buyer, as he is a seller from another. He buys the goods of the other party, and he sells his own. But, in order to avoid inconvenience, the transaction is generally effected by means of money; and similarly, from the point of view of economic theory, it is easier to look at only one side at a time.   And so for the term *value* it is convenient to substitute the term *price*, by which, as Mill points out, the "value of a thing in relation to money" is meant, and to regard the party offering the money as a *buyer*, and the party offering the goods as a *seller*.

The theory of value assumes that the exchange is freely made, and that competition is active on both sides; and, since Mill wrote, the term *market* has been defined with greater exactitude by Jevons as expressing, not necessarily a particular locality, but a district stretching, it may be, over a whole country, where, as regards any particular trade or

[1] Marshall's *Principles of Economics.*

commodity, competition is fully and freely operative, communication is easy and rapid, all sellers know the terms on which other sellers are selling, and all buyers are acquainted with the conditions under which other buyers are purchasing. A *market*, in the economic sense of the term, is a sphere within which there is only one price for the same amount of the same quality of the same commodity ; and the assumption of perfect competition which this definition implies has been brought into more distinct prominence since Mill's time.

In such a market, again, it is assumed that there will be a *normal* or *natural* price. There will be a price at which the competition of buyer with buyer, and seller with seller, will be always tending to make buyer and seller arrive. There may be temporary deviations from that price ; but, so long as competition is active, it must be the centre to which these deviations tend to return. The theory of value was considered by Mill to be concerned in the main with the influences affecting this *normal* price ; but the recent course of economic inquiry has tended to distinguish with greater emphasis than he may be said to have employed the temporary or *market* from the *normal* or natural price ; and it has also exhibited the mutual influence exercised by the one on the other.

The influences affecting this *normal* price may be regarded from the side of the sellers, or from that of the buyers ; and, to make the theory complete, the results separately obtained must be combined together. Later economic study has tended to show the advantage of dividing the inquiry, and to emphasise the mutual dependence on one another of the influences which are operative on either side. It has laid greater stress on those affecting the buyers than Mill was

perhaps inclined to do ; for, like his predecessors, he devoted
more pains to investigating the motives determining the
action of sellers.

The obvious fact with regard to the *sellers* is that they
will not continue to produce at a loss. They will endeavour
to realise such a price at least as will cover the cost they
have incurred in order to place the goods on the market.
They will, it is true, be individually anxious to secure a
higher price; but, assuming that competition is active,
were one of their number to endeavour to obtain this higher
price, his competitors would, in their anxiety to secure a
larger proportion of the custom, offer to sell at a lower price,
and underbid him.   He would be forced to bring down his
price to their figure, and this would be the lowest price
which would not result in loss.   If it were higher, fresh
capital and labour would flow into the trade in pursuit of
these advantages, and, in their eagerness to secure part of
the custom, the new producers would offer successively at
lower figures until they reached this point.   For the competition assumed in the theory is not merely that of dealer
with dealer, but also that of producer with producer; and
Cairnes, who emphasised the distinction, defined the two
varieties respectively as *commercial* and *industrial* competition.   The *normal* price, then, is that which will recoup
the *cost of production.*   It cannot be lower in the long run,
for producers will not continue to produce at a loss ; and
it cannot be higher, for otherwise fresh competitors will
enter the trade.

Later economic study has disclosed some advantage in
the substitution of the term *expenses of production* for that of
cost of production which Mill employs ; and the advantage
appears on an analysis of the terms.   By the term *expenses*

of production is meant such a remuneration for the effort of labour, and the abstinence, or postponement of enjoyment, implied in the accumulation of capital, required for the production of the commodity, as is considered to be *normal.* It implies *wages* and *profits* paid to the workmen, and to the employers and capitalists, who have co-operated in the production of the commodity, of such an amount that, were they lower, some workmen, and some employers and capitalists, would withdraw their labour and capital from this particular trade, and seek more advantageous employment elsewhere, and, were they higher, some workmen, and some employers and capitalists, would leave some less advantageous industry and seek employment here. In the term *profits* are included the profits of the producer himself, and of all who have in any way contributed to the production of the commodity. The term *wages* is employed in a similarly comprehensive sense; and the *expenses of production*, which the *normal* price must recoup, comprise also such occasional items as taxes and the like. Nor should it be forgotten that the expectation of competition from outside is often sufficient to lower the price. The fresh capital and labour need not actually come into the industry : it is enough that producers expect that it will.

So far Mill's analysis of what he calls the *cost of production* is in general agreement with this account, although he did not explicitly draw the distinction between the employer and the capitalist, which has been specially emphasised since his time by the American economist President Walker, or lay any such stress on the separate importance of the component parts of what is commonly understood by *profits.* But he seems to have used the term *cost of production* in two senses. Sometimes it means the

money wages and profits of different occupations, and
sometimes the actual effort of labour, and abstinence from
expenditure, or postponement of it, of which these wages
and profits are the money rewards. Later economic inquiry
has explicitly distinguished these two meanings; and the
term *expenses of production* has been introduced to mark the
former, and the term *cost of production* confined to the latter
meaning. This correction of Mill's phraseology has been
due in a large measure to the emphasis laid by Cairnes
on the fact that, if *industrial* competition is not fully
realised, wages and profits in different occupations may
not be an equivalent reward for the labour incurred,
and the abstinence from expenditure, or the postponement
of it, undergone by workmen and capitalists[1] in their
respective trades. Some workmen may earn more, and
some capitalists less, than others in return for the same
amount of effort and abstinence. There may be *non-competing groups* of labourers, between which competition is not
thoroughly active, and labour does not freely move, leaving
the less and passing into the more advantageous occupations.

On this point Cairnes, following with apparent uncon-
sciousness in the steps of Mill, who had noticed the fact,
divided industrial society into four rough grades; but later
inquiry has compared it rather to a staircase with different
landings. There may be grades of industry, and sub-divisions
of those grades; and between the sub-divisions in each
grade labour may move with comparative freedom, but not
between the grades themselves. The professional classes may,
for all practical purposes, be a *group* with which, save in
exceptional cases, skilled workmen do not compete. They

---

[1] Cairnes did not distinguish between employers (as such) and
capitalists (as such).

could not enter the professions, if they would ; for they have not the requisite education or social position. Nor again can there be any doubt that one of the most difficult barriers to pass is that which in modern industrial society separates the skilled artisan from the unskilled labourer. And similarly, though this point was not noticed either by Cairnes or by Mill, who failed to distinguish the functions of the employer as such from those of the capitalist, large capitalist-employers may have a certain advantage over their smaller rivals which is not removed by competition. The difficulty of administering larger amounts of capital may not increase proportionally to the increase of that capital ; and yet, as Professor Sidgwick shows,[1] it is generally held that the component parts of profits advance and decline equally with one another, and that the *wages of superintendence or earnings of management*—the remuneration, that is, of the employer, as such— vary with the amount of capital administered and *interest* received.

In these cases, where competition is not sufficiently powerful to remove, or pass over, the barriers which intervene between different *groups*, the real *cost of production* may differ from what are now distinguished as the *expenses of production*. But here, as before in the case of *price*, money must be employed for purposes of comparison. It is impossible to compare directly effort with effort, or abstinence with abstinence : they can only be compared indirectly through the money remuneration they usually secure. The *normal price* of a commodity, therefore, is now said to represent its *normal expenses of production*.

The term *expenses of production* requires, however, further analysis ; for the circumstances and conditions of production

[1] *Principles of Political Economy*, Bk. II. ch. ii. § 8.

may vary in the case of different commodities.   There may
be some of which the expenses *do not vary with the amount
produced.*   It might be difficult to name any particular
commodities of this class, and Mill's description of the conditions of their production is not very explicit.   But undoubtedly there are commodities which belong to the other
two classes which he distinguishes.   There are *articles of
rarity,* such as fine pictures and scarce books, which are
limited in quantity; and there are commodities, like
agricultural produce, of which beyond a certain point, owing
to the operation of the law of diminishing returns, an increased amount can only be produced at an *expense per item
which increases more rapidly.*   There is, lastly, a class of
commodities which Mill might perhaps have done well to
substitute for that which was mentioned first.   It consists
of commodities, such as *manufactured articles,* a larger production of which means a *decreased expense per item.*   Division
of labour can be carried to a greater extent, and various
economies effected.

In the last two cases the *expenses of production*, which will
determine the *normal* price, will be those of that portion
of the commodity for which there is a demand, the *expenses
of production* of which are the greatest.   It will be so ; for,
were it not, some producers would fail to clear their expenses, and would be tempted, or compelled, to abandon
production.   As respects these two cases, then, which comprise the majority of commodities, a larger production
implies, from the point of view of the seller, in the one a
higher and in the other a lower price, and diminished production *vice versâ* in the one a lower and in the other a
higher price.   And so, before we can determine these
marginal expenses, as we may call them, or expenses on the

margin of production, which the *normal* price must recoup, we must know the quantity of the commodity which is demanded. We are forced to inquire into the circumstances affecting *demand,* and to investigate the *buyers'* side of the question.

It is on this side that the later development of the theory has been most marked; and Mill does not seem to have given adequate recognition to the influence of demand on the circumstances of supply. He was aware that the chief condition, which was needed to occasion a demand for a commodity, was that it should possess some *utility*, and conduce to some purpose, or satisfy some desire. If indeed it could be obtained for nothing, and its production involved no expense, no one would be willing to give anything in exchange for it. But, supposing that it cost something to produce, and presented some *difficulty of attainment*, it was still necessary that it should possess some *utility*. It was according to this *utility that the* demand varied; for, the greater the utility, the greater would be the demand, and, the less the utility, the less also would be the demand. Buyers would give more for what they wanted, and less for what they did not.

The general law, which regulates demand, was recognised by Mill; but it has since been stated with greater precision, and developed more fully. It is that, the larger the quantity a man already possesses of a commodity, the less is likely to be the *utility* to him of an additional quantity. The less he is willing to give of other commodities in exchange for it; and, therefore, the larger the supply of any commodity, the lower, from the point of view of the buyers, is likely to be its price. The suggestive expression *final utility* has been used by Jevons to illustrate this obvious inclination of human nature, and the alternative expression *marginal utility* has been substituted by a more recent writer.[1]   By the *final* or *marginal utility* of a commodity is meant the utility of it as measured by that of just that last portion for which the buyer is willing to give the price asked rather than go without it.   If the price were slightly raised, he would prefer to dispense with that last portion; and, if it were lowered, he would purchase a little more.   The whole of the commodity which is bought has a value or utility to the buyer; and this was what Mill called its *value in use*. It denotes the total amount of satisfaction derived from its enjoyment, or, in other words, its *total utility*.   But this particular last portion has a particular value, by which the *final* or *marginal utility*, or, as Mill would call it, the *value in exchange*, of the commodity, is determined.   It is this *final utility* which determines the *normal price* from the side of the buyers.

From the point of view, then, of the sellers, the *normal price* represents the *expenses of production*, and these vary in most cases with the amount demanded.   From the point of view of the buyers it represents the *final* or *marginal utility*, and this varies with the amount supplied.   In the majority of instances, accordingly, demand and supply are mutually determined, and Mill does not seem to have recognised this interdependence with sufficient distinctness. But there are some cases in which they are not thus determined.

If the *expenses of production* of a commodity are fixed in the sense that no more of it can be produced, its price will be determined from the point of view of the buyers rather than that of the sellers, by the influences affecting demand

---

[1] Professor Marshall in his *Principles of Economics*.

rather than those affecting supply. The sellers will not, indeed, willingly consent to receive less than will cover their *expenses of production ;* but, so far as fresh competition on their side is concerned, they may obtain a much higher figure. The price will depend on the *final* or *marginal utility* of the commodity to the buyers. They will not pass beyond this point, but they may be compelled to go as far. They may be forced to offer as much as they would be willing to do rather than dispense with the commodity. This is the case with *articles of rarity*, such as fine pictures, or sculptures, or old books ; and Mill's explanation of this class of commodities may perhaps be considered adequate, although it has not the advantage of the more precise terminology and detailed analysis of later writers.

If, again, the *expenses of production* of a commodity are fixed in the sense that any additional amount of it can be produced at an *unvarying expense per item*, the price will be determined from the side of supply, and all that demand will do is to settle the amount produced. The price cannot rise above, or fall below, the *expenses of production*, so long as competition is freely and fully operative. It was to this class of commodities that Mill accorded a very large space in his exposition ; and hence, probably, it was that he gave too exclusive an emphasis to the influence of *cost of production* on the normal price. For the sake of theoretical completeness such a class should be considered, but it would be difficult in practice to particularise the commodities belonging to it. The error of Mill seems to have lain in his failure to make an explicit application to the theory of value of what he had elsewhere shown to be the advantages attending the increased production of manufactures.

The largest classes of commodities are probably those of which the *expenses of production per item diminish or increase with the amount produced*, and it is under the first of these two classes that those *manufactured commodities* should be properly placed, which Mill put into the class which has just been considered. The second of the two classes includes *agricultural produce*. In the case of both classes, the *normal* price is the result of the mutual play of demand and supply. In either case, from the stand-point of the buyers, the law of demand holds good that, the greater the amount of the commodity offered for sale, the less will tend to be its *final* or *marginal utility*, and the lower its price ; and, on the other hand, the smaller the quantity offered for sale, the greater will tend to be its *final* or *marginal utility*, and the higher its price. But the question becomes more complex when it is regarded from the stand-point of the sellers. In the case of *manufactured commodities* the *expenses of production per item* tend to diminish as the amount produced increases ; and, therefore, the greater the amount demanded, the lower will be the price at which each item can be offered for sale, and, the smaller the amount demanded, the higher must be the price. In the case of *agricultural produce* the circumstances of production incline in the opposite direction, and the resulting conditions of sale are altered. In both cases, then, varying considerations have to be taken into account, and all that can be positively stated is, that the *normal price* must be such as to equate the demand with the supply forthcoming at that price.

This *normal price*, then, is not one single price ; for the quantity supplied, as well as the quantity demanded, may alter with it. At a higher price less of the commodity might

be demanded, for its *final* or *marginal utility* would diminish ;
but, if the commodity belonged to the class of *manufactured
commodities*, the *expenses of its production* might also be such
as to necessitate, with a decreased production, a higher
price, and thus the new price might, like the old, represent
the *marginal expenses of production* to the sellers, and the
marginal or *final utility* of the commodity to the buyers.
At a lower price, again, the buyers might be willing to
purchase more, and this extension of demand might permit
of diminished *expenses of production per item*, for it might
allow of increased division of labour with its attendant
advantages. And so here again the price might represent
the *marginal expenses of production* to the sellers, and the
marginal or *final utility* of the commodity to the buyers.
But it would be a different price from that realised before,
although, like that, it would be a *normal* price. Recent
economists have drawn a distinction more explicitly than
Mill had done between an *extension* of demand of this
nature, resulting from a fall in price, and a *rise* of demand
betokening an increase in the amount demanded of the
commodity at a given price. Mill did not state this distinction with such explicitness, or emphasise the possibility
of two or more *normal* prices ; but he seems to have been
conscious of the distinction, and in his exposition of international value he definitely recognised the possibility. The
work of later writers has often consisted in rendering
explicit what is only implicitly contained in his exposition.

Much of that work, however, has been of importance ; and
it has helped to accomplish what Mill himself failed to
effect. He did not realise, or at any rate he did not
exhibit, the harmonious development of the theory of value
in its full and varied application. He laid the foundations,

and in the main he laid them truly and well; but he did not rear the complete superstructure. His work was transitional.

He recognised, for example, the existence of market values as affected by temporary and special circumstances; and he instituted an instructive comparison between value and the sea, which, with a surface which is "always ruffled by waves, and often agitated by storms," "everywhere tends to a level," and "never is at an exact level." But he did not show, what later inquiry has emphasised, the inter-action of *market* and *normal* values. They are chiefly distinguished by the comparative length of the periods of time over which they extend; but the starting-point of investigation must in either case be the mutual play of *demand* and *supply*, and it is only by analysing supply that we reach that *cost of production*, which is given so prominent a place in Mill's exposition as the determining cause of *normal value*. He did not adequately show how it was influenced by demand, the law of which is similar for *market* and *normal values*.

Nor, again, did he fully recognise the closeness of the connection between the theories of *domestic* and *international* value. His treatment of the two is distinct, and yet the play of demand and supply must be present in both, and furnish the starting-point of investigation. Nations are indeed, so far as the movement of labour from the less to the more advantageous employment is concerned, con-spicuous examples of *non-competing groups;* but capital exhibits every year less unwillingness to migrate from country to country, and the idea of *non-competing groups* is not entirely foreign to markets which are confined to the geographical limits of a single country. The tendency of subsequent inquiry has been to show the similarity of the two theories, and to discover the operation of similar laws in both, although the particular conditions of their application may differ, and the *cost of carriage* to the market be a more important element in international than in domestic trade.

Thirdly, and lastly, Mill did not apply his theory to the exchange of services. He did indeed extend the application of it step by step from other commodities to money, and from money in domestic trade to money as a factor of the foreign exchanges; and the development he thus traced in the successive chapters of his third book was admirably systematic. Nor are his allusions to wages and profits in these chapters open to much criticism; but he never brought the theory of distribution of his second book into harmony with his theory of value. Later inquiry has taken this important step, and shown how the theory of value applies to the determination of interest, profits, and wages, as well as prices. The terms on which capitalists will exchange their capital for the labour of employers and workmen, and the terms on which employers and workmen will exchange their own services in the production of wealth for those of one another, are held to be determined by influences affecting demand and supply. There are *market* rates of interest, profits, and wages, due to transient and special circumstances, and extending over periods of time which are relatively short; and there are *normal* rates, to which these *market* rates tend in the long run to conform.

A capitalist will not obtain a higher rate of interest for the loan of his capital than that which represents the *marginal utility* of the capital to the borrower; and he will not in the long run be content with a lower rate than that which will satisfy the postponement of enjoyment which its

I

accumulation has involved. A skilled workman will endeavour in the long run to secure for his services a wage which will repay the *expenses of production* of his skill—the expenses, that is, of his rearing and training—and, if he did not succeed in this endeavour, the supply of skilled workmen would in time fall off. But the employer on his side will not be willing to give higher wages than those which represent the *marginal utility* of the service to him, and the position of the workman and the capitalist with regard to his earnings of management will be similar. The more scarce, again, a service is, and the greater its *utility*, the higher will be the reward it will tend to secure; and the smaller its *utility*, and the more abundant it is, the lower will be its reward.

The *normal prices* of services are thus, like those of commodities, determined by the mutual play of demand and supply; and among the influences affecting supply the *expenses of production* occupy a predominant place. Perhaps the main defect of Mill's exposition is his failure to recognise this; although the fact should never be forgotten, which his separate treatment tends to emphasise, that there are elements connected with human feelings and affections in the exchange of services which do not enter into the exchange of inanimate commodities.

CHAPTER V.

JOHN ELLIOTT CAIRNES. 1824—1875.
THOMAS EDWARD CLIFFE LESLIE. 1827—1882.

ECONOMIC METHOD.

Mill's Predominance—His Successors and Critics—Cairnes' Life—His Courageous Endurance of Physical Pain—The Character of his Writings—Their Defects—His *Slave Power*—His *Essays on the Gold Question*—His Deductive Method of Investigation.

Cliffe Leslie's Life—His Criticism of the Deductive Method—The Advantages of Both Methods, (1) the Abstract and Deductive, (2) the Inductive and Historical—The Relation of Economics to Sociology—The Special Advantage of the Historical Method in placing in their Right Setting the 'Exploded' Theories of the Past —The Usury Laws.

In the last chapter the position of Mill in the history of English Economics was brought under review. We saw that his work was transitional; and that the theory of value, which he held to be 'fundamental,' and to be presented in its final shape in his treatise, had since been criticised from various stand-points, and developed in different directions. For some years, however, after the publication of his *Principles*, it seemed as if his exposition of political economy, like that of Ricardo before him, would be unquestioned. Bagehot has described[1] his influence as 'monarchical,' and remarked that modern students, instead

[1] *Economic Studies*, p. 215.

of beginning with the older economists, approach them through the medium of Mill, "and see in Ricardo and Adam Smith what he told them to see."

But, after a lapse of some twenty years, his supremacy was disturbed. The assault came from various quarters, and was not in every case intended. Mill himself in 1869, in a review of W. T. THORNTON's book *On Labour*, abandoned[1] the wages-fund theory, which he had previously accepted and explained. Jevons in 1871 published a *Theory of Political Economy*, in which he expounded, and illustrated by the aid of mathematics, that conception of '*final utility*' which was noticed in the last chapter. He supplemented rather than refuted Mill, but he represented his own position as widely divergent; and, in a preface to the second edition of his book, he declared that he was "ever more clearly coming" to the "conclusion." "that the only hope of attaining a true system of Economics" was "to fling aside, once and for ever, the mazy and preposterous assumptions of the Ricardian school." "That able but wrong-headed man, David Ricardo, shunted the car of Economic science on to a wrong line, a line, however, on which it was further urged towards confusion by his equally able and wrong-headed admirer, John Stuart Mill." In 1874 Cairnes issued a book on *Some Leading Principles of Political Economy newly Expounded*, in which he, like Jevons, supplemented Mill's theory of value, especially by the emphasis which he laid on that conception of '*non-competing groups*' which has already been explained. But, like Jevons also, he represented Mill's attitude on some points as approaching absurdity, although he avowed himself to be his disciple. In 1870 Cliffe Leslie began a

[1] See Mill's *Dissertations and Discussions*, vol. iv. pp. 43, etc.

series of attacks on the abstract Ricardian method from the general stand-point of the German historical school of economists; and, finally, in 1876, in some articles in the *Fortnightly Review*, which were published, together with other material, after his death in *Economic Studies*, Bagehot sought to limit the application of the Ricardian theories to the facts of business life in large trading communities like England.

In these various ways the predominant influence of Mill was impaired; and the fabric, which had been cemented together by him, and built up on the foundations laid to some extent separately, and to some extent jointly, by Adam Smith, Malthus, and Ricardo, was closely inspected, unsparingly tested, and partly reconstructed. The period has been one of development and criticism; and, although Fawcett, in his *Manual of Political Economy*, which was originally published in 1863 before Mill's pre-eminence had been disputed, was content to reproduce in the last of the six editions through which it successively passed during his lifetime very nearly the same summary of Mill's *Principles* as that which he had furnished in the first, in this respect he stands outside the general line of development of economic thought, and it is only now that it is beginning to be possible to gather up and combine into an orderly and harmonious whole such results of the criticism and extension of Mill's doctrines as may be considered to be approved. This work has been recently attempted by PROFESSOR MARSHALL in his *Principles of Economics*.

The contributions made by two of Mill's successors to the advancement of economic study will occupy our attention in subsequent chapters. In one we shall examine that description of banking and the money-market,[1] with which the name of Bagehot is associated; and in the other[2] we

---

[1] Chapter vi.   [2] Chapter vii.

shall give an account of the work of Jevons on that statistical side of economics, to which he felt himself most powerfully attracted. The present chapter will be especially concerned with the discussion of the method appropriate to economic inquiry; for such a discussion will naturally arise in connection with the work of Cairnes and Cliffe Leslie. They occupy the opposite poles of the question, and the one was a supporter and example of the deductive, while the other was an advocate and illustrator of the inductive or historical method.

The life of JOHN ELLIOTT CAIRNES furnishes a remarkable instance of the power of a resolute will to overcome physical difficulties. During his later years he suffered from a malady, of which the severity continually increased, and death was the only possible termination. He was born in Ireland, at Drogheda, in 1824, and, after leaving school, spent some time in the counting-house of his father's brewery. His tastes, however, inclined in another direction, and he entered Trinity College, Dublin. He then engaged in the study of law, and was called to the Irish bar, but for many years he was chiefly occupied in writing articles for the press. He devoted great attention to Political Economy, and made the acquaintance of ARCHBISHOP WHATELY, who had himself been Professor of the subject at Oxford,[1] and had founded a chair in Trinity College. In 1856 Cairnes was appointed to this chair, and in 1858 and the two following years he wrote a series of articles on the probable results of the recent discoveries of gold in California and Australia. In 1861 he was appointed Professor of Political Economy in Queen's College, Galway, and a course of

---

[1] Whately's Lectures were published in 1831. He proposed to call Political Economy " Catallactics, or the Science of Exchanges."

lectures, which he delivered here, formed the basis of his book on *The Slave Power.* It was published at a critical juncture in the American Civil War, and, although opposed to the general drift of influential opinion in England, secured a wide repute. In 1865, when he was forty-one years of age, his illness began with an attack of inflammatory rheumatism, from which a speedy recovery was at first confidently anticipated. But these hopes were disappointed, and the disease steadily advanced. In 1866 he was appointed Professor of Political Economy in University College, London; but he was compelled to pass the session of 1868-69 in Italy, and in 1872 to resign the chair. In 1875 he died at the early age of fifty-one.

The disease from which he suffered was one of which the severity was continually increasing, and it was impossible to foresee the full extent. It was a malady of the most discouraging nature. Joint after joint was attacked, and the movement that could barely be effected one month was impossible the next. First Cairnes would walk, we are told,[1] with the aid of crutches; then he would be wheeled in a chair; then the shaking of the chair would become intolerable, and he would only be carried out now and again into his garden. At last even this was abandoned, and for some time before his death he never left the house at all. He was gradually reduced to a state of helplessness more complete than that of an infant.

And yet these years of intense physical suffering were years of great intellectual activity. During this period he prepared and published his largest work on *Some Leading Principles of Political Economy;* and he collected and re-arranged his scattered writings in two volumes, one of

---

[1] By Fawcett, in an article in the *Fortnightly Review* for 1875, vol. xxiv.

which was entitled *Political Essays,* and the other *Essays in Political Economy, Theoretical and Applied.* He preserved such ' charm ' of conversation, ' vivacity, and humour,' that his friends used to reserve their choicest jokes for him, feeling sure that he would evince the keenest relish in them, and looked forward to their talks with him as some of the brightest moments of their lives. His interest in contemporary politics was keenly maintained, and he united with this a power of abstract reasoning, which has seldom been equalled, and perhaps never surpassed, for clearness and firmness. Indeed, so clearly did he apprehend, and so firmly did he grasp one side of a question, and so luminous and forcible was his exposition, that he sometimes produced on his readers the impression that there could not possibly be another side or a different opinion. He seems, from the very strength of his intellect, and the energy of his will, to have been unable to enter fully into the point of view of an opponent; and this sometimes rendered him an unfair controversialist, although no unfairness was intended.

His largest economic work affords an illustration. *Some Leading Principles of Political Economy* is divided into three parts, the first of which is devoted to Value, the second to Labour and Capital, and the third to International Trade. The most important portion of the book, regarded as a contribution to the development of economics, consists in his examination of the theory of value. It is here that he puts forward the conception of ' *non-competing groups.*' But the force with which he urges the conception, and the vigour with which he maintains his position, create the impression of a more fundamental correction of Mill's theory than he seems to have really made. It is true that he calls emphatic attention to cases where ' industrial competition' is not completely realised, and labourers do not freely move from the less to the more advantageous occupation in sufficient numbers to render the remuneration of labour in different trades an equivalent to the effort which is respectively required. This failure of competition may, as he shows, occasion a divergence between the real *cost* and the nominal *expenses* of production[1]; but on the one hand he appears, with all his intentions to the contrary, to have led many of his readers to conceive the barriers separating these ' *non-competing groups* ' as more rigid and impassable than they actually seem to be, and, on the other, to have failed to indicate an alternative means of comparing effort with effort to that furnished by the money-remuneration they respectively obtain. He wrote out, in fact, one side of the question in a bold clear hand; but his argument lays stress on a qualification of Mill's theory rather than, as he seems to think, demonstrates its absurdity. It emphasises the important consideration that competition is not always fully operative, and that a theory based upon competition may need modification; but it exhibits some tendency to introduce into that modification the very absoluteness which it condemns in the theory.

In the same way, the criticism which he passes on Jevons' conception of *final utility* seems to show that he had not fully grasped its meaning; but he undoubtedly contributes some luminous suggestions to the elucidation of the principles which he 'newly' expounds, and his illustration of abstract theory by actual fact is often opportune. He shows, for example, that the recorded transactions and observed

---

[1] See above, p. 104. Cairnes himself did not use the expression *expenses of production ;* and Senior had anticipated the distinction which he establishes.

phenomena of commerce have confirmed the theory of
international value, and the conception of international
trade, which economists have formed by abstract reasoning.

It is this capacity for disentangling, and exhibiting, the
operation of a principle amid an intricate mass of complex
facts which constitutes his greatest intellectual gift ; and
his book on *The Slave Power* is the most notable, and
perhaps the most enduring, example of it.   It seems to
be that one of his writings on which his fame may eventually
rest ; and even so hostile a critic as Cliffe Leslie has declared that it "will ever defy criticism," while another writer
has described it as "one of the finest specimens of applied
economical philosophy." In it he endeavoured to predict from
the known effects of causes known to be present the events
of the future, and he applied considerations based partly
on speculative reasoning to the elucidation of a practical
problem.

He investigated the economic influence of slavery on the
course of civilisation.   The advantages of slavery as a
'productive instrument' were 'comprised' in the 'absolute
power' of the employer, and the consequent opportunity
for organisation.   But its economic disadvantages were
three in number.   Slave-labour was 'given reluctantly';
and the industrial operations of slaves must be concen-
trated on a small space within reach of the superintendence
of a few overseers.   The slave was 'unskilful,' and, so far
from having any inducement to acquire intelligence, he was
kept in compulsory ignorance for fear of rebellion ; and,
therefore, the industry on which he was engaged must call
for little or no skill.   Thirdly and lastly, he was wanting in
'versatility,' and it was difficult enough to teach him a
single trade ; and so his work must be uniform.

The cotton industry of the Southern States of North America fulfilled these conditions ; but it did so at the cost of serious injury to civilisation. The want of skill and versatility forbade rotation of crops, and implied a constant abandon_ment of exhausted soils, which fell into a desert condition, and became the haunt of the 'promiscuous horde' of the 'mean whites.' And it also implied a continual acquisition of fresh fertile land at the expense of more civilised and industrious neighbours. The same deficiencies of slave-labour prevented the growth of manufactures or commerce, and compelled the planters to obtain the capital needed for working their large plantations by incurring debt.

And such a society might continue to exist, owing to the modern facilities of intercourse ; for, through the international division of labour, it might obtain the products of the skilled industry of other countries in exchange for its own, while the lands too exhausted for cultivation by slave-labour might be profitably devoted to the breeding of the slaves themselves. Just as an "anatomist" might be "able," Cairnes remarked, "from a fragment of a tooth or bone to determine the form, dimensions, and habits of the creature to whom it belonged," so might a "political economist, by reasoning on the economic character of slavery and its peculiar connection with the soil, deduce its leading social and political attributes, and almost construct, by way of a priori argument, the entire system of the society of which it forms the foundation."

It is by a similar exhibition of the working of a principle amid a mass of facts that his Essays towards a Solution of the Gold Question are characterised. He traced the "consequences which would result from" "the increased supplies of gold," which were pouring into the world from the mines of California and Australia, "supposing all other things to remain the same." He was aware that the "actual course which phenomena" táke is the "composite result of the combined action of many" influences; but, for the purpose of effective inquiry, he isolated the one cause of which he endeavoured to deduce the probable effects. It had been commonly thought that a "depreciation of money could only show itself in an uniform action upon all prices;" but he "ventured to combat" this view, and to "state the mode and order in which the monetary movement, as it proceeded, would be developed." He showed that the prices of those articles, and those countries, with which the fresh supplies of gold first came into contact, would be first and most fully affected, and that the effects would be transmitted at a later time in a subordinate degree to other commodities and countries. He thought that the rise in price would be more rapid in raw materials than in manufactured commodities, because the latter could respond more readily to the stimulus to increased production afforded by the abundance of money and the expectation of the rise of price; and, for similar reasons, he thought that, amongst raw materials, the rise would be greater in the case of "animal products" than those of "vegetable growth." He thought that the productions of England and the United States would experience the rise in the first instance after the commodities produced in the gold countries themselves, and then the productions of the continent of Europe, and lastly those of India and China, in consequence, partly of the relative extent of their dealings with the gold countries, and partly also of the relatively expansive capacity of their currencies, according as they did, or did not, consist largely of "credit contrivances."

The method of investigation thus employed by Cairnes in the cases of slavery and the gold discoveries was the method which he regarded as appropriate to economic inquiry. In his book on the *Character and Logical Method of Political Economy*, which originally consisted of a series of lectures delivered in Dublin as Whately Professor in 1857, but was revised in 1875 immediately previous to his death, he elaborately discusses the point. He defines Political Economy as "the science which, accepting as ultimate facts the principles of human nature, and the physical laws of the external world, as well as the conditions, political and social, of the several communities of men, investigates the laws of the production and distribution of wealth, which result from their combined operation." "The phenomena of wealth, as they present themselves to our observation, are," he remarks, "amongst the most complicated with which speculative inquiry has to deal. They are the result of a great variety of influences, all operating simultaneously, reinforcing, counteracting, and in various ways modifying each other." If the political economist "declines to avail himself of any other path than that of strict induction, he may reason till the crack of doom without arriving at any conclusion of the slightest value." He must employ the "method of deduction" "incomparably, when conducted under the proper checks, the most powerful instrument of discovery ever wielded by human intelligence."

This deductive method was vigorously assailed by the writer whose work we have now to examine. THOMAS EDWARD CLIFFE LESLIE was, like Cairnes, an Irishman by birth. He was born in 1827, and educated, first by his father, then by a clergyman at Clapham, and finally at

King William's College in the Isle of Man. But, when he was only fifteen years old, he entered Trinity College, Dublin, where Cairnes was also at this time a student. After the conclusion of his college course he studied law at Lincoln's Inn, attending the lectures of Sir Henry Maine, to whom he confessed his indebtedness for the knowledge of that "historical method of investigation," which he carried over himself from the sphere of jurisprudence, to which Maine had applied it, into that of political economy. He was called to the English bar, but in 1853 was appointed Professor of Jurisprudence and Political Economy in Queen's College, Belfast. He visited Ireland from time to time to discharge the duties of his chair ; but he continued to live in London, making frequent journeys to the Continent for purposes of economic observation, and contributing largely to the periodical press on economic subjects. For some years he suffered from a painful malady, which occasioned his death in 1882, at fifty-four years of age. He had apparently planned a systematic treatise on English economic and legal history; but the manuscript was lost in 1872, and his contributions to economics consist almost entirely of two volumes of collected essays, one of which was published in 1870 on the *Land Systems and Industrial Economy of Ireland, England, and Continental Countries*, and the other in 1879, under the title of *Essays on Political and Moral Philosophy*. The latter of these two volumes has been recently re-issued, with the omission of some of the more general essays, and the addition of others on strictly economic topics.

The work of Cliffe Leslie is negative rather than positive ; and, in spite of the acuteness and vigour with which he assails the deductive method and the abstract reasoning of the so-called 'orthodox' school of economists, his criticism can scarcely be considered destructive. He argues that the economic view of man and society can only be parted by an arbitrary separation from the other aspects from which man and society are regarded. The present state, as the future condition, of any particular country is the outcome of a long process of historical evolution, in which moral, political, legal, and economic forces have acted and reacted in inseparable union, and combined to produce indistinguishable results. The motives influencing the conduct of men are many and varied, and are ambiguously described by economists as the 'desire of wealth.' The 'average rate of profits and wages' is a misleading expression, and should be replaced by a detailed inquiry into the many different actual rates.

"Political economy," he writes, "is not a body of natural laws in the true sense, or of universal and immutable truths, but an assemblage of speculations and doctrines which are the result of a particular history, coloured even by the history and character of its chief writers." The "abstract, *à priori*, and deductive method" "throws" "hardly any light on the nature of wealth," of which "there is a multitude of different kinds" "differing widely in their economic effects." "The desire of wealth is a general name for a great variety of wants, desires, and sentiments, differing widely in their economical character and effects." "In every country instead of an average or common rate of wages there is a great number of different rates, and the real problem is, 'What are the causes which produce these different rates?'" "The truth is, that the whole economy of every nation, as regards the occupations and pursuits of both sexes, the nature, amount, distribution, and consumption of wealth, is the result of a long evolution, in which there has been both continuity and change, and of which the economic side is only a particular aspect or phase. And the laws of which it is the result must be sought in history and the general laws of society and social evolution." "Every successive phase of social progress presents inseparably connected phenomena to the observation of the economist, the jurist, the mental, the moral, and the political philosopher." "Political economy is thus a department of the science of society which selects a special class of social phenomena for special investigation, but for this purpose must investigate all the forces and laws by which they are governed." "Political Economy has not reached the stage of a deductive science," "the fundamental laws of the economic world are still imperfectly known," and "can be fully known only by patient induction."

The positions thus adopted by himself and Cairnes on the question of the appropriate method of economic investigation are diametrically opposed. Unlike Cairnes, he examines the rise of prices by a separate investigation of detailed facts in different countries and districts; and he conducts on similar lines an inquiry into the "movements of agricultural wages." But later study seems to have proved that there is room for both methods. There are departments of Economics, where the arrangement and collection of facts are specially appropriate, and Professor Sidgwick has shown[1] that the production of wealth has usually been treated by an inductive method comparing and generalising from observed facts. It is in the department of the distribution and exchange of wealth that a different method has been adopted; and it is difficult to see how it

[1] *Principles of Political Economy*, Introduction, ch. iii.

could with advantage have been otherwise.   Bagehot has said [1] that, " if you attempt to solve such problems " as the " facts of commerce," present "without some apparatus of method, you are as sure to fail as if you try to take a modern military fortress—a Metz or a Belfort—by common assault ; you must have guns to attack the one, and method to attack the other."   And he has shown that in other sciences than Political Economy progress has been made by considering the "effects of one particular set of causes by themselves," by imagining hypotheses, and deducing the results of these hypotheses.   It is true that the hypotheses should be carefully framed to correspond as closely to facts as possible, and that the results deduced from them should be constantly compared with the results of actual experience, and the divergence clearly exhibited and diligently examined.   But, without the aid of theory, it is impossible to proceed; for, as Professor Marshall argues,[2] "facts by themselves are silent."   It is precisely because many different objects of many different desires are embraced, as Cliffe Leslie shows, under the term ' desire of wealth,' that the assumption made by economists of the universal character and unlimited extent of the ' desire of wealth ' in general is broadly true, though it would be untrue of each particular desire for each particular kind of wealth.   It is because Cairnes considers the action, and deduces the results, of an isolated cause, while Cliffe Leslie starts with the detailed examination of a multitude of facts, that the former exhibits the rise of prices occasioned by the increased supplies of gold in a luminous and intelligible order, and the latter seems scarcely to " see the wood for the trees."

[1] *Economic Studies*, p. 10.   [2] *Principles of Economics*, p. 74.

K

But the inductive and historical method has its place and value. It tests and corrects the foundations and the conclusions of the abstract deductive method. It shows that the theories of the older economists were sometimes stated too universally, at any rate by more extravagant followers, and that they require modification when employed as explanations of actual fact. Cliffe Leslie maintained that some of Cairnes' speculative predictions respecting the depreciation of gold had not been exactly verified by subsequent experience; and he laid stress on the obstacles which limit in practice the complete attainment of an uniform average rate of profits or wages. Cairnes, although he recognised that an economic 'law' was nothing else than the statement of what would follow from certain assumptions,[1] was perhaps inclined to under-rate the advantage of bringing the results of these laws to the test of comparison with fact; and Cliffe Leslie supplied the needful corrective of reference to actual experience.

But he proceeded to the opposite extreme; and sometimes he almost denied the possibility of an economic 'law,' or the benefit of a working hypothesis. Nor is that interdependence of social phenomena, on which, following Comte, he insists, very helpful in the absence of an 'unified social science.' Social phenomena may, as he shows, be connected together; but the progress of scientific inquiry has been mainly due to a separation of the problem into its component parts, and a distinct investigation of each. The economist should undoubtedly have regard, as he urges, to the other sides of society, and to its influence as a whole; but he may advantageously isolate, for the purposes of inquiry, the material and industrial side, and consider chiefly

[1] See below, Chapter viii., p. 188.

the motives determining the action of individuals. The
work of historical economists has called attention to these
other aspects, and to the influence of special historical ante-
cedents and social surroundings on the complexion of facts
and the formation of theories; and Ricardo and the
economists of his time were inclined to generalise unduly
from the character of the 'city' men they knew themselves.
They thought that man was invariable and unchangeable;
and the historical method offers a needful caution against
applying conclusions based upon men, as they are at one
time, under one set of circumstances, to men as they are at
another time, under another set of circumstances.

Perhaps, however, its especial use has been to mitigate
the condemnation which might otherwise be passed on the
mistaken theories of by-gone ages. By the very importance,
which it tends to give to facts, it shows how a different set
of facts may have given rise to a different set of theories.
Facts which are now prominent may have been then in the
background, and facts which are now in the shadow may
then have been in the light. With our modern knowledge
and experience, for example, we think it foolish and mischievous to prescribe a legal maximum rate of interest,
beyond which no one may legally lend or borrow. We
argue that the effect of such a law is, not to prevent the
needy man from borrowing at a higher rate, but to make
him pay still more, to compensate the lender for the risk
which he runs of being detected by the law, and losing both
interest and principal. We point to the means by which
such laws could be evaded, and we contend that it is better
to leave matters to the ordinary market influences, making
stringent provisions, and devoting our efforts to the enforcement of these provisions, against violence and fraud. And

so we pass an unqualified condemnation upon the Usury Laws.

But if, with such an historical economist as DR. CUNNING-HAM in his *Growth of English Industry and Commerce*, or PROFESSOR ASHLEY in his *Economic History*, we shift our stand-point, and go back in imagination to the state of mediæval society, and supply the circumstances of historical fact amid which these laws were enacted, we begin to ;qualify our condemnation.   We see that there was no such opportunity for the investment of capital as there is now, and that the possessor of a large sum of money could scarcely apply it to any productive enterprise or use it himself in such a way as to realise a profit.   If, then, he lent it, and the security were good and the money repaid, he rendered a service to another man, but sustained no loss himself.   Nor was it the prosperous who would borrow, but the poor in distress, to relieve whom was the Christian duty of the rich.   To ask, then, for more than the simple repayment of loans appeared to be extortion, and plainly immoral.

In this way the historical method conduces to a more tolerant judgment on the ' exploded ' theories of the past ; and the facts which its advocates have generally examined have hitherto been mediæval facts.   So far as the analysis of the present is concerned the quarrel between the abstract, or deductive, and the historical, or inductive, economists does not appear to be based on any very real foundation, and seems to be now abating.   Cliffe Leslie himself observes of Roscher, the most distinguished of those German economists whose method " is the investigation of the actual course of history, or the historical method," as opposed to the English method " of proceeding by deduction from certain postulates or assumptions," that the "difference between Ricardo's work on the *Principles of Political Economy* and Roscher's, lies rather in the amount of historical research in the latter than in fundamental diversity of doctrine," and that "so far as doctrine is concerned the difference is for the most part one more of tone than of principle, and often makes itself felt chiefly in the absence of dogmatic formula, and of the use of rigorous and infallible logic affected by Ricardo's school." When the difference is reduced to this narrow compass a fitting summary of the whole question may perhaps be found in Bagehot's remark [1] that "rightly conceived the Historical method is no rival to the abstract method rightly conceived."

[1] *Economic Studies*, p. 15.

CHAPTER VI.

WALTER BAGEHOT. 1826—1877.

THE MONEY MARKET.

A Difficulty of Political Economy—Bagehot as (1) a Man of Business—
and (2) a Student—His Writings—His Imaginative Powers—His
Phrase-Making—His Descriptive Ability—His *Lombard Street*—
The Era of the 'Great Commerce'—The English Banking System
—(1) Its Power—*Lombard Street* as a 'great Go-between'—(2) Its
Delicacy—The Bank of England as the Keeper of the One Cash-
reserve—The Reasons for its Pre-eminence—Different Origins and
Functions of Banks—(1) Negotiating Loans—(2) Supplying Good
Money—(3) Remitting Money and (4) Issuing Notes—(5) Receiving
Deposits—Danger of the English System at a Time of 'Commercial
Crisis'—Differences between Old and Modern Trade—The Elas-
ticity of Credit—The Urgency of the Demand for Cash—The Bank
Charter Act—A 'Panic must not be Starved'—An Escape from
the Dilemma—The Effects of Raising the Rate of Discount—Con-
flicting Interests of the Bank Directors—Subsequent Changes.

THE author, whose contributions to the development of
economics in England will occupy our attention in this
chapter, remarks in a passage of his writings that political
economy has one " inherent difficulty," "which no other
science" "presents in equal magnitude." "It is an
abstract science which labours under a special hardship ";
and that hardship consists in the circumstance that "those
who are conversant with its abstractions are usually without

a true contact with its facts," and "those who are in contact with its facts have usually little sympathy with and little cognizance of its abstractions." It is an 'analysis' of the world of business; and economists are seldom themselves men of business, and have to obtain their facts second-hand, while men of business, who know the facts, seldom, if ever, reason about them, or at any rate do not reason precisely. They act by instinct more than by argument, and they would be sorely puzzled to put into scientific language the origin, the course, and the results of their action. "And so the 'theory of business' leads a life of obstruction, because theorists do not see the business, and the men of business will not reason out the theories."

But Bagehot himself might be quoted as an instance of an economist who combined in his own person these desirable qualifications. He was a man of business and a student; and it is probably for this reason that he has sketched with a surer hand than perhaps any other writer the connection and the distinction between economic theory and the facts of every-day life. In his *Economic Studies* he has shown that the theory is limited in its application, that it starts from certain assumptions which should be tested by reference to fact, and that, reasoning from these assumptions, it reaches conclusions which should be brought to a similar test. But he has also shown that the theory is necessary, because we could not without its aid arrange the 'complex' facts of the business world in any intelligible order, or prepare practical problems for wise and reasoned solution.

He was, then, a man of business as well as a student. He was a man of business by descent, connection, and occupation. He was born at Langport, in Somersetshire, in 1826, and was the only surviving child of a father, who, as Mr. Hutton states,[1] was "for thirty years Managing Director and Vice-Chairman" of Stuckey's Bank, and, before he retired from his post, "the oldest joint-stock banker in the United Kingdom." His mother was the niece of the founder of the bank, Mr. Samuel Stuckey; and Bagehot himself, abandoning the idea he had entertained, after concluding his course of study at University College, London, of practising at the Bar, succeeded his father as Vice-Chairman of the Bank; and maintained to the end of his life that "business" was "much more amusing than pleasure." His marriage in 1858 to the daughter of Mr. James Wilson, the founder of the '*Economist*' newspaper, resulted in his becoming editor of that paper; and in this position he had to keep in close and constant touch with 'city' men and 'city' talk.

To this editorial connection we may perhaps ascribe two consequences. It made him cultivate a habit of writing in such a way as to be understood by plain practical 'city' men; it made him select with this object the most appropriate and striking language, even if it was sometimes almost ungrammatical; it made him determine to be at all costs interesting. And it also led him to devote attention to the working of the Money Market, his description of which we may select for especial consideration, as forming his most complete contribution to economics. As a banker he had already been forced to study it on its practical side; and now as the editor of a financial newspaper he was compelled to inquire into its theoretic bearings. Mr. Giffen

---

[1] In a Memoir prefixed to Bagehot's *Literary Studies*.

declares[1] that he seemed to know by "instinct" "what the business man would do"; and, although to the end of his life he could not bring himself to deal with *minutiæ*, to add up columns of figures, or to correct printers' proofs, he is said to have possessed in a remarkable degree what has been aptly called a "quantitative sense." He knew how far the business man would go on a certain line of conduct, and at what point he would be likely to stop.

But he was also a student; and in many respects he had more of the student in him than of the man of business. His success as an economist was largely due to the knowledge which he brought from outside to bear on his economic writings; for he was a student with a considerable range of study. The titles of his books illustrate this. Besides his economic writings, which comprise a little book on the subject of an *International Coinage* or *A Universal Money*, some articles on the *Depreciation of Silver* reprinted from the *Economist* in 1877, some essays, partly fragmentary, on the nature and limits of political economy and the characteristics and work of the early English economists, and a description of the Money Market in a book entitled *Lombard Street*, he has left behind him an account of the *English Constitution*, in which he examines its character and working with keen insight and graphic force. He has also written some *Essays on Parliamentary Reform*, which were republished before the recent extension of the franchise; his *Literary* and *Biographical Studies* furnish abundant evidence of wide and appreciative reading, and acute and discriminating criticism; and his book on

---

[1] In an article in the *Fortnightly Review* in 1880 on *Bagehot as an Economist*.

Physics and Politics is described by himself as a collection of "thoughts on the application of the principles of 'natural selection' and 'inheritance' to political society." Mr. Hutton maintains that his "most original writing," as an economist "was due less to his deductions from the fundamental axioms of the modern science, than to that deep insight into men which he had gained in many different fields." In his own nature the "man of business and the financier" fell within "sharp and well defined limits"; and "he knew better than most" economists "where their special weakness lay, and where their special functions ended." Mr. Giffen declares that he was not "primarily an economist," but "primarily a man of letters of strong genius and imagination, who happened amongst other things, and subordinate to other things," "to take up with Political Economy."

This description of him as a "man of letters of strong genius and imagination," brings into deserved prominence what was perhaps his most striking characteristic; and it was a characteristic which contributed greatly to his interesting, and almost fascinating, treatment of economic subjects. "He always talked, in youth, of his spirits as inconveniently high"; and throughout his writings the reader feels that he is in contact with a 'buoyant' and 'subtle' imagination. His conversation is described as 'racy'; and his phraseology is habitually and instinctively vivid. One of the chapters in his book on *Lombard Street* bears the title: "Why Lombard Street is often very dull and sometimes extremely excited"; and it is scarcely possible to read a page of his writings without coming across some apt and striking phrase which lingers in the memory. His definition of a "constitutional statesman" as "in general a man of common opinions and uncommon abilities," his description of "savages" as "playing" the "game of life with no knowledge of its rules," and his account of the Cabinet as the "hyphen" joining the "legislative part of the state to the executive part," are some among many examples which might be quoted.

To this vivid imaginative power, which betrayed itself alike in his high spirits, his racy conversation, and his incorrigible habit of phrase-making, we may ascribe two characteristics of his writing. To his nature "the commonest things often seemed the most marvellous, and the marvellous things the most intrinsically probable." His vivid imagination rendered him also an admirable describer of concrete phenomena. His strength, indeed, seems rather to have lain in description in "bold and broad" outline than in elaborate reasoning or exhaustive analysis. But his work as a describer was of a high order, for he possessed in an eminent degree the quality of 'detachment of mind.' Mr. Hutton declares that this quality was so marked in him that it "tended to give the impression of" "intellectual arrogance," and that he was comparatively inaccessible to the "contagion of blind sympathy." But it was owing to the same quality that he showed himself to be a cool and critical observer, and an accurate and impartial describer ; and he preferred to describe in the concrete wherever he could. There are traces of observation of the "actual world of politics" in his *English Constitution*, there is evidence of insight into men and manners in his *Physics and Politics*, and similarly his *Lombard Street* is described as being as "much a study of bankers and bill-brokers, as of the principles of banking."

It has been said that this last book is perhaps the most

finished in form of Bagehot's writings. He wrote it not
long before his death, which occurred suddenly from disease
of the heart in 1877, when he was only fifty-one years of
age.   In some respects his powers were at their best when
he composed the book, and throughout its composition he
kept steadily before his mind two aims which he was
specially fitted to realise.   He endeavoured to impress both
men of business and literary students ; he wrote alike for
the practical man and the theorist.

In his *Physics and Politics* he calls attention to the changes
which had passed over the complexion of society during the
previous fifty years, and to the "new world" of "inventions" and "ideas" which had "grown up" during that
period.   It was especially to the facts of this new world,
and, in a less degree, to the circumstances of English
economic history during the whole period which had elapsed
since the occurrence of the great industrial changes at the
close of the last, and the opening of the present century,
that, in his opinion, the science of political economy was
strictly applicable ; for it was the "science of business, such
as business" was, "in large productive and trading communities" like England.   It was "an analysis of that world
so familiar to many Englishmen—the 'great commerce'
by which England" had "become rich."   And one of the
characteristic features of that world, as it was one of the
most necessary parts of the mechanism of that 'great
commerce,' was the Money Market, as it is described in
Lombard Street.

It was, he maintained in his *Economic Studies*, possible to
go back to a "pre-economic age" long previous to that
'great commerce,' and long before Ricardo or Malthus or
Adam Smith, when the assumptions of political economy

would be untrue to fact. In such an age one of these assumptions would be untrue, because there was, speaking generally, no "transferability of labour" from the less to the more advantageous employment. There were no "employments" between which labour could move, for the structure of early society was rigid and "uniform." There was no "strong government" to preserve domestic peace, or prevent foreign attack; and the institution of slavery, like that of caste, hampered man's freedom of choice. Nor would another assumption of modern economics be true to the facts of early society, for the "transferability of capital" would not then be realised. There were no "trades," in which profits could be made, or between which capital could move, and there was no money-medium, by means of which profits could be compared, or capital "held in suspense."

But, in the world of the 'great commerce,' on the other hand, there was, he maintained, transferability of labour, and, in a higher degree, transferability of capital. There was the "loan-fund of the country lying in the hands of bankers and bill-brokers which" moved "in an instant towards a trade" "unusually profitable, if only that trade" could "produce securities which" came "within banking rules." There was a "great speculative fund," "composed of the savings of men of business" and others, ready to flow into promising undertakings; and there was, lastly, the "obvious tendency of young men starting in business to go into the best-paying" and most likely business.

Of these three agencies, tending to withdraw capital from the less and bring it into the more profitable undertakings, the first and, in a smaller measure, the second, are perhaps the most effective and wonderful; and it is in England that they have brought, as Bagehot shows, to the greatest perfection in the development of the banking system. This it is which is the most conspicuous and necessary part of the mechanism of the 'great commerce'; and it is one of those common things which to Bagehot seemed the most marvellous, and of it he gives an account in *Lombard Street.*

He begins his book by describing Lombard Street as " by far the greatest combination of economical power and economical delicacy that the world has ever seen." Money,[1] as every one will admit, is "economical power," and " England is the greatest moneyed country in the world." " It has much more immediately disposable and ready cash than any other country." We have abandoned the idea that " any undertaking likely to pay, and seen to be likely, can perish for want of money "; and it has been said that "any foreign country can borrow in Lombard Street *at a price* "—possibly high or possibly low.

That this is so is the result of our banking system. Englishmen are accustomed to keep a banking account, but they do not often concern themselves to ask what it is that the banker does with their money. He keeps, it is true, a portion ready at hand to meet the ordinary daily demands of his depositors, and, by dint of long experience, he can ascertain with tolerable assurance what that portion should be at different times. But the rest of the money he lends out at interest, it may be to merchants and manufacturers, or it may be to landlords and farmers; and in this way he assists the general industry, and promotes the commercial prosperity, of the country.

[1] He here uses 'money' in one common acceptation of the term to denote what might be more accurately termed ' borrowable capital'; another is to denote merely coin or bank-notes.

But, as Bagehot points out, if the district in which he lives is "purely agricultural," he may be unable to employ with advantage all the money deposited with him, which he can safely lend out. And so he hands over the disposal of the money he cannot himself employ to his London agent, or a London bill-broker, and they in their turn lend it to the great industrial centres. It is in this way that the deposits in the different banks constitute a great 'loan-fund,' and that the controlling centre of this fund is to be discovered in Lombard Street, where some of the chief London bankers and bill-brokers have their places of business. Lombard Street is, as Bagehot phrased it, the "great go-between." "It is a sort of standing broker between quiet saving districts of the country and the active employing districts." It is the locality where, in an especial degree, we may say that the most powerful and delicate part of the mechanism of the 'great commerce' is situated, for it is the home of the Money Market.

London is thus a place where money is always obtainable. It is through the agency controlled in Lombard Street that capital moves rapidly in England from the less to the more profitable trades, that a new and active trader acquires the control of the capital which enables him to compete success-fully with the old and established trader, who works with his own, and not with borrowed capital, and that English com-merce and manufacture are marked by a 'democratic structure' and a ceaseless activity. It is owing to the same agency that "all *sudden* trades come to England," where there is this means of getting 'new' men and 'new' capital into a trade, and that England retains her command over 'old' trades, to which she might seem less naturally suited than other countries. And hence it follows that all theories of the overthrow of her commercial and manufacturing supremacy require revision in the light of these circumstances.

But the mechanism is as 'delicate' as it is 'powerful,' and Bagehot wrote his book to show that it had its special dangers as well as its peculiar advantages. He pointed out that besides the ready cash, which the country banker finds it necessary to keep by him in actual coin or bank-notes in his till, in order to satisfy the ordinary daily demands of his depositors, he generally has somewhere or other a 'reserve,' on which he can draw with ease and rapidity should he have to face some unusual demand. Most of the money deposited in his hands is deposited 'at call,' or 'short notice,' that is to say, it can be demanded at once or after a brief delay; and there may be occasions when people will not rest content with anything else but actual coin, or legal tender of the realm, and will look askance at such paper-promises to pay as are furnished in cheques and bills of exchange. And so somewhere or other in the banking system there must be a cash-reserve.

Under our system this reserve is kept in the Bank of England. The country bankers keep their cash-reserve with their London agents, and the London bankers keep theirs at the Bank of England. "It may be broadly said," Bagehot writes, "that no bank in London or out of it holds any considerable sum in hard cash or legal tender (above what is wanted for its daily business) except the Banking Department of the Bank of England." "The same reasons which make it desirable for a private person to keep a banker make it also desirable for every banker, as respects his reserve, to bank with another banker if he safely can; for "the custody of very large sums in solid cash entails" of necessity "much care and some cost."

And hence it is that the Bank of England is the 'Banker's/ Bank.' It keeps the cash-reserves of the London banks and bill-brokers, and also, directly or indirectly, of the country banks of England, Scotland and Ireland; and it has even become, to some extent, 'the Banker's Bank' of Europe.

In a country town cheques drawn on a local banker are accepted in payment of debts, and in London those drawn on a London bank are taken, while the London banks themselves settle any difference, which may be found at the 'Clearing House' between the cheques in their possession drawn on some particular bank and the cheques drawn on themselves in the possession of that particular bank, by a cheque drawn on the Bank of England. And, as Bagehot went on to show, foreign countries resort in their turn to London for money; and London, receiving more than any other place, and paying more than any other place, on account of the extensive sale of English manufactures abroad, and the considerable purchase of foreign goods by England, becomes the natural financial centre of Europe, and the Bank of England keeps to some extent the cash-reserve of Europe. Thus the proportion of cash to the liabilities resting upon it becomes 'exceedingly small;' and a kind of hierarchy is established in the banking world, with the Bank of England in the position of pre-eminence. The mechanism controlled in Lombard Street is as 'delicate' as it is undoubtedly 'powerful.'

But these considerations suggested the question: Why had this pre-eminence fallen to the lot of the Bank of England? Bagehot answered it by giving an account of the origin and development of banking. The English banking system, familiar and common as it might seem, was in reality

one of those common things which were 'most marvellous.'
No such developed system existed in any Continental
country; and the original motives, which had led to the
foundation of banks, were in many cases unlike the later
uses to which they were applied.

The early banks of Italy, where the name seemed to have
originated, were simply 'finance companies,' started to
effect loans for the governments of the mediæval republics.
And this was the original function of the Bank of England
itself; for it was started by the Whig government of William
III. in order to obtain money from the subscribers to carry
on the war with France.   The government of the Restoration had undermined credit, and destroyed confidence, by
appropriating the 'reserve of treasure' deposited in the
Exchequer by the goldsmiths, who were the bankers of those
times, so far as they discharged that function of banking
which consisted in the safe custody of valuables.   In 1694
the credit of William III.'s government was so low that it
could not "borrow any large sum"; and a plan was accordingly devised by which, as Macaulay stated, some twelve
hundred thousand pounds were to be "raised, at what was
then considered as the moderate rate of eight per cent.,"
and the subscribers were to be incorporated under the
name of the 'Governor and Company of the Bank of
England.'

It was in a more 'curious' fashion that the great banks
of the north of Europe originated.   Adam Smith had
described how, at the time of the commercial supremacy
of the Dutch, the "extensive trade of Amsterdam" brought
to that city a "great quantity of clipt and worn foreign
coin," and the value of the currency fell some "nine per
cent. below that of good money fresh from the Mint."

He had told how, in "order to remedy" the "inconveniences" and uncertainty which were consequent upon this, a "bank was established in 1609 under the guarantee of the city," which "received both foreign coin, and the light and worn coin of the country at its real intrinsic value in the good standard money of the country, deducting only so much as was necessary for defraying the expense of coinage, and the other necessary expense of management. For the value which remained" "it gave a credit in its books"; and "this credit was called bank money," and "represented money exactly according to the standard of the mint." All bills above a certain value had by law to be paid in this "bank money," and every merchant, therefore, was compelled to "keep an account with the bank." Its function, then, was primarily to provide good money; and this function may also be said to belong, in a sense, to the Bank of England, which acts as the agent of the Mint in the receipt of bullion and the issue of coin.

A third and "most important" function of early banks was that of "remitting money" from place to place; and in these various ways they acquired the confidence of those with whom they had transactions. They came to be known and trusted, and men were ready to deposit their money in their hands. But there was a yet more important way in which they brought themselves under the notice of a wider circle; and that was the supply of a paper currency, such as the bank-notes issued in England. Bagehot declares that this seems to have been the chief means by which banking develops and bankers become known, and are trusted with the deposits of others. Nor is the reason, he thinks, far to seek; for a bank can issue notes more easily than it can obtain deposits. "To establish a note

circulation, a large number of persons need only," he writes,
"*do nothing*. They receive the banker's notes in the
common course of their business, and they have only *not*
to take those notes to the banker for payment." But an
" effort " is needed in the case of deposits, and the action of
the depositors is no longer passive. And hence it is
that in banking history the issue of notes has generally
formed the prelude to the receipt of deposits. It encourages
deposits; for, "when a private person begins to possess a great
heap of bank-notes, it will soon strike him that he is trusting
the banker very much, and that in return he is getting
nothing. He runs the risk of loss and jobbery just as if
he were hoarding coin. He would run no more risk by the
failure of the bank if he made a deposit there, and he would
be free from the risk of keeping the cash."

Now, the Bank of England, Bagehot proceeded to argue,
owed its pre-eminence partly to the fact that it was closely
associated with the Government, which gave it the " exclusive
possession " of its balances, and the humbler citizen was
content to follow the example of the Government which
must know better than himself. And, again, it was partly
owing to the circumstance that it " had, till lately, the
monopoly of limited liability in England," and its directorate
was joined by " many quiet and careful merchants," " who
certainly would not have joined any bank where *all* their
fortunes were liable, and where the liability was not limited."
But, over and above these undoubted advantages, it had the
especial "privilege of being the sole *joint-stock company*
permitted to issue bank-notes in England "; and the clause
in the Act of 1742, which conferred this privilege, was for
some time construed as if it carried with it the exclusive
right of receiving deposits. In this way the Bank of

England acquired the monopoly of the note-issue in the metropolis of a country, which, unlike most Continental countries, had enjoyed a long period of exemption from the danger of invasion or revolution, and had therefore had time for a note-issue to become trusted and popular. "Inevitably it became *the* bank in London; all the other bankers grouped themselves round it, and lodged their reserve with it." That was the history of the banking hierarchy, and the reason why in England, unlike America and other countries, there was one instead of several cash-reserves.

And now that the system had grown up it was difficult to alter it. But the pre-eminence of the Bank carried with it a serious responsibility; and it was Bagehot's opinion that, whatever might, or might not, be the 'practice' of the Bank directors, in 'theory' at least they did not recognise this responsibility. It was true that in ordinary times the duty, which devolved upon them, of administering the cash-reserve was not so grave and onerous; but it was when a panic had arisen, and when a commercial 'crisis' was at hand or in progress, that the duty became critical and absorbing. To explain why this was the case he wrote perhaps the most important and interesting chapter of his book: "Why Lombard Street is often very dull and sometimes extremely excited."

There may, broadly speaking, be said to be two main differences between trade, as it was conducted before the modern era of the 'great commerce,' and trade as it is now carried on. Before that time the producer of commodities was more generally known to the consumer, and more frequently met his demands as they arose. Now the consumer may be at one side of the globe, and the producer

at the other ; and errors may arise regarding the kind and
amount of particular commodities for which there is at any
particular time a real demand.   Too much of one or of
several commodities may be produced, and too little of
others ; and thus some industry, or group of industries, may
be depressed.   And it may hand on part of this depression
to other industries, or groups of industries, whose products
it consumes.   For there is, as Bagehot termed it, a 'partnership' in industries.   In brisk times one industry communi-
cates its briskness and prosperity to another ; and in seasons
of dullness and depression one industry 'propagates,'
through a variety of others, its dullness and depression.
And all this takes time : the full effects of the 'calamity'
cannot be experienced at once, and the recovery from it is
slow and gradual.   Hence it is that trade ebbs and flows,
and flows and ebbs ; and there are alternating periods of
prosperity and adversity, of brisk trade and dull trade,
of 'good times' and 'bad times.'   At one period the
industrial and commercial mechanism is in perfect order,
and is working with the maximum of speed ; at another
that speed is slackened, or the machine thrown out of gear.

All these effects are intensified by the presence in modern
industrial society of an element at once wonderfully effective
and marvellously delicate, which was comparatively unknown
before the era of the 'great commerce.'   That element is
credit.   A great amount of trade is now carried on by
means of borrowed capital.   The deposits in the bankers'
hands constitute a large 'loan fund' ready to move in
any direction where there may be favourable openings.   A
banker becomes a " kind of 'solvency meter,' " showing what
men may be trusted with borrowed money, and how far
that trust may go ; and a "very great many of the strongest

heads in England spend their minds on little else than on thinking whether other people will pay their debts."

In brisk times the expansion of credit is at once a sign and a promoting cause of the briskness. There is a more active spirit of confidence abroad. Trade is said and felt to be prospering : prices are reported to be rising. And so people are encouraged to spend and buy, and sellers are ready to trust for payment at a future date. Merchants are willing to 'draw' and 'accept bills,' bankers and bill-brokers are ready to 'discount' them, and to use the capital placed at their disposal by their depositors to supply the merchants or manufacturers who draw, and the merchants or manufacturers who accept, the bills with additional capital. And thus a vast system of credit is built up on a slender basis of actual cash. People are ready to lend, and speculators are anxious to borrow. Prices rise, and especially the prices of articles which form 'fixed capital,' like machinery and buildings, railways and ships, which are urgently needed to help in producing and carrying to the consumer the goods so urgently demanded, and cannot be at once supplied.

But this very activity is likely to set in operation forces which tend to produce depression. Fixed capital takes some time to yield a return, speculation is carried to excess, bubble companies are started, speculators are forced to sell and thus lower prices ; and a feeling of discouragement begins to spread. Some one perhaps at this juncture fails to meet his engagements, and discharge his paper-promises to pay. He is ruined ; and a feeling of distrust follows on that of discouragement. These feelings are very contagious ; and the characteristic feature of such a commercial crisis is that credit contracts as rapidly as it has previously expanded.

For at such a time people want hard cash, or 'legal tender'

of the realm, and they will not be content with paper-promises to pay that hard cash or legal tender.   They want something that will discharge debts, or that has intrinsic value of its own, or that can be at once converted into something possessing intrinsic value.   Bankers are chary of discounting bills, depositors are tempted to withdraw their deposits, merchants and manufacturers are disinclined to sell goods on credit, speculators are unwilling to invest.   The one thing wanted is hard cash, or legal tender; and the only place where it can ultimately be obtained under our banking system is the Banking Department of the Bank of England.   It is there that the cash-reserve of the nation is kept, and that the real basis of the fabric of credit is to be found.   If the country banker anticipates a 'run,' or fears that the demands of his depositors for coin or notes will be more than usual, he tries to strengthen his cash-reserve, and calls on his London agent to help him.   But that London agent cannot meet an unusual demand from his own resources, for he keeps his cash-reserve at the Bank of England; and so the drain ultimately comes upon the Bank of England.   If a foreign country, again, wishes to withdraw part of the reserve it keeps in London, its demand must ultimately be met from the same source; for that is the only cash-reserve of the nation.

It is, as Bagehot pointed out, in the Banking Department alone that it can legally be met.   By what is known as the Bank Charter Act of 1844, the Bank of England was separated into two distinct departments, of which the Banking Department was to carry on the ordinary business of a banker, and the Issue Department was to issue bank-notes alone.   The Act was passed with the intention of guaranteeing the convertibility of bank-notes into gold;

and the Issue Department was allowed to issue notes up to fourteen millions, and two-thirds of the lapsed issues of country banks, on the basis of government securities, part of which was formed by the debt of the Government to the Bank. This sum was supposed to represent the amount of notes, which would normally remain in circulation, and not be presented for payment; and beyond this amount the department was only to issue notes on the basis of actual bullion deposited in its cellars. Its action in the matter becomes automatic, giving gold in exchange for notes, or notes for gold; and all that the Banking Department can legally obtain from it in seasons of pressure is one form of legal tender in exchange for another. It cannot increase its reserve of legal tender by drawing on the bullion in the cellars of the Issue Department; nor can it strengthen its position by the sale of government securities, for they are not what people want. By whatever road we travel, we are brought back to the conclusion that the pre-eminence of the Bank of England carries with it a serious responsibility, for it is the sole custodian of the only remedy which is effective at critical junctures. As Bagehot puts it, "on the wisdom of the directors of that one joint-stock company it depends whether *England shall be solvent or insolvent.*"

The gravity of the situation was, he pointed out, enhanced by some further considerations. As a panic arose from men thinking that there would not be sufficient cash for all, and that they must anticipate others in securing some for themselves, if they were to avoid ruin, the surest way to increase a panic was to occasion an idea that the amount of cash available was less than had been thought, and the only means of arresting it was to create a impression at an early stage that it was larger. A panic was, in fact, "a species of neuralgia, and according to the rules of science you must not starve it." The holders of the cash-reserve must be ready to advance it freely in times of panic. They must lend to merchants, manufacturers, bankers, and bill-brokers, "'to this man and that man,' whenever the security is good."

It would seem, then, as if the Bank directors were impaled on the horns of a dilemma. A sufficient supply of ready cash is the one thing needful, and yet those who have the control of the single cash-reserve must be prepared to diminish it. They must, it would appear, be ready to cut away the ground from beneath their feet. But there is a means of escape from the dilemma. The reserve must be replenished before the panic comes; and the alarm which then prevails is, as Bagehot shows, often so unreasoning, that it may be allayed in a manner which might seem to be as unreasonable. It is only needful to lend a little at an early stage to create the impression that money is, and always will be, available. And that little may be lent at a high rate of discount; for all that is wanted is to "diffuse" the notion that, "although money may be dear," it "is to be had." The panic of 1836 subsided "after a day or two" of lending on the part of the Bank, and the panics of 1847 and 1866 were arrested by the rumour that the Chancellor of the Exchequer had given power to the directors to suspend the Bank Charter Act, and to issue an additional number of notes.

But this does not absolve the Bank from the duty of watching its reserve in times of prosperity, and strengthening it when it is likely to be needed. The greater part of the deposits in banks is held on "short notice," if not on "demand," and "the owners could ask for it all any day they please." But the amount of cash compared with the fabric of credit which rests upon it is far from great, and the natural consequence follows that the diminution of the reserve will awaken the gravest apprehensions, if it is frequently allowed to become very small.

The Bank directors had, as Bagehot pointed out, an effective means of replenishing the reserve. They could advance the rate of discount, and raise the terms on which they were willing to lend money. By this course of action they diminished their liabilities at home and abroad. They induced foreigners to send money to reap the benefit of the high rate of discount at which it could be lent; and they occasioned a tendency to a fall in prices by discouraging speculation, and increasing the difficulty of borrowing. Foreign countries would, therefore, prefer to send bullion here rather than goods, and to take goods from here rather than bullion, as money was worth more, and goods could be purchased cheaper.

But, although it was now the actual practice of the Bank directors to replenish their reserve in this way, yet, Bagehot argued, they did not recognise the maintenance of a sufficient reserve as part of their bounden duty, and on the three occasions when the Bank Charter Act was suspended—in 1847, 1857, and 1866—the suspension was considered necessary because the Banking Department was practically empty, and the directors had allowed the reserve to be drained away.

Nor was this, in his opinion, unnatural. The directors were not, and did not consider themselves to be, government officials. They were not even bankers by profession; for no banker as such could sit on the directorate, although a bill-broker might. Nor were they pecuniarily much interested in the fortunes of the bank, for their liability was limited. They were simply "rich City merchants," chosen with great care. And they were the representatives of shareholders, who would suffer in their pockets by a diminution of the discounting business of the Bank, and were placed at a disadvantage compared with other joint-stock banking companies, which kept their reserves at the Bank of England and avoided the trouble and expense of keeping reserves of their own. Nor had those shareholders any fear of impairing the credit of the Bank by diminishing the reserve, for it was the common idea that the Bank could not fail.

The Bank directors were, then, placed in such a position that the influences, which might naturally be supposed to have weight on their minds, would lead them to diminish rather than maintain the reserve. But they possessed one advantage, which they have now to a considerable extent ceased to retain. The rate of discount was settled by the action of demand and supply in the Money Market, and money was a "commodity subject to great fluctuations of value" caused by a "slight excess" or "deficiency of quantity." The Bank of England occupied the position, no longer of a "predominant," but of a "most important dealer in money," for part of the money which it could supply was necessary. And so the rate of discount at which it was willing to lend settled the maximum, and influenced the general, rate in Bagehot's time.

But now the general rate seems to have passed further away from its control. Private banks have diminished in number and influence, but joint-stock banks and bill-brokers have grown. The bill-brokers may be said to settle the rate of discount, and the leading London banks, who are now practically on an equality with the Bank of England, place their surplus cash with them. And hence the bill-brokers and the joint-stock banks regulate the demand for money, and the power of the Bank of England over the rate of discount tends to decline. But it continues to be the trustee of the cash-reserve; for neither the bill-brokers nor the London banks keep reserves of their own, but are professedly dependent for cash on the Bank of England. Responsibility is thus divorced from power, and the characteristic danger of the Money Market is increased. Its recent history has illustrated this; but it has also shown that, in a large measure owing to Bagehot's forcible pleading, the consciousness of the delicacy of the English banking system is more fully and generally felt, and the directors of the Bank of England are in practice, if they are not in theory, more ready to appreciate the responsibilities of their position as the custodians of the one cash-reserve. The main contentions of *Lombard Street* may be said to have become "part of the accepted theory of banking"; and may lead, at no great interval of time, to important changes.

CHAPTER VII.

WILLIAM STANLEY JEVONS. 1835—1882.

STATISTICS.

THE economist, whose work we are now about to con-sider, refers in one of his letters to an ambition which he had felt in early life. " If there were one thing," Jevons writes, " I should wish to be, it would be a recognised statistical writer." This youthful aspiration was fulfilled. A competent judge of his statistical writings has declared that the "pure honesty" of his "mind, combined with his special intellectual fitness for the work, have made them

models for all time."[1] It is true that he is not known
merely for his statistical studies; for he was a logician of a
high order, and an economist of great and varied ability. But
it is also true that, on the one hand, the logical character of
his mind combined with his extensive knowledge of general
economic subjects to produce his excellence as a statistician,
and, on the other, that that part of his work seems to have
presented the greatest attractions to him, which lent itself
the most easily to treatment of a statistical nature.

He became a statistician of the first rank ; and his qualities
were such as to ensure this result. The reader of his *Theory
of Political Economy*, in which in 1871 he explained, and
applied to the theory of value, the conception of final utility,[2]
must be sensible that, bold as his theoretical reasoning is,
he owed much of its exactitude to a keen appreciation of
fact. If, on the other hand, we turn to that book on *The
State in Relation to Labour*, which was published in 1882,
or to those essays on the *Methods of Social Reform*, which
were collected in a volume after his death, we recognise
that his wise and sympathetic treatment of such practical
problems as the "amusements of the people," the employment of "married women in factories," and the advantages
of a "state parcel post," was due, in some measure at least,
to his firm grasp of theory. PROFESSOR FOXWELL has said [3]
that "in his union of high speculative ability with the greatest
reserve and sagacity in the treatment of practical problems,"
he was a "conspicuous example of the truth" of the defence
of theoretical study made by the French economist Cournot,
who urged that "those who are most concerned for the

[1] Professor Marshall in the preface to Jevons' *Investigations in
Currency and Finance*, p. xliii.
[2] See above, page 107.   [3] In the preface mentioned above, p. xlii.

precision of their principles will be most sensible of the limits of their application, and therefore the least unpractical in their treatment of real questions."

It was this combination of qualities which rendered him so able a statistician. A reproach is frequently levelled against statistics, which is summarily expressed in the statement that "figures will prove anything"; but it is justified only by their misuse, and this may be traced in a large measure to an unnatural divorce of theory from facts, or facts from theory. The assertion " simply means," as MR. GÖSCHEN states,[1] that "figures, which never tell untruths, may be so handled as to present untruths." There can be little doubt, however, that the view of statistics, which is commonly prevalent, is unsatisfactory; and MR. GIFFEN has remarked [2] that in "journals of the highest standing there are the wildest blunders of the schoolboy order." This misuse and misrepresentation may perhaps be ascribed to two main causes, one of which is the comparatively recent date of any scientific treatment of the subject, and the other consists in the many serious difficulties which attend such a treatment.

It is true that in one sense, as the French statistician and economist M. Block has observed, statistics "have existed ever since there were States." The name seems to have originally referred to "inquiries into the condition of a State"; and Achenwall, who has been called the "father of modern statistics," regarded [3] them as a "survey of the customs, laws, and forms of government, by which one

[1] In his inaugural address as President of the Royal Statistical Society in 1887. Mr. Göschen is the author of a work on *The Theory of the Foreign Exchanges*, which has passed through many editions.

[2] *Essays in Finance* (second series), p. 133.

[3] See Du Guy's paper in the *Jubilee Volume of the Royal Statistical Society*. Achenwall lived from 1719—1772.

nation differed from another"—as history, in short, with the uninteresting details, as they seemed to him, of the names of monarchs, the changes of dynasties, and the issues of wars, left out. He did not dwell so much on their numerical as on their descriptive character; but they are now generally understood to mean collections of facts capable of expression in a numerical and, if possible, tabular form. This was once known as 'political arithmetic;' and SIR WILLIAM PETTY,[1] two centuries ago, described his essays at this 'arithmetic' as the use of a "method" "not yet very usual," which, instead of employing "only Comparative and Superlative words and Intellectual Arguments," enabled him to "express" himself in "Number, Weight, and Measure." In similar language Jevons characterised a series of statistical papers, which had been collected by him, and were published after his death under the title of *Investigations in Currency and Finance*, as an "attempt to substitute exact inquiries, exact numerical calculations, for guess work and groundless argument."

Even in this latter meaning of 'political arithmetic' statistics have an ancient origin. It has been said that almost the first act of a regular government would be to number its fighting men, and the next to ascertain the amount of taxation which could be raised from the rest of the community. But it is apparently[2] only within the last three hundred years that systematic scientific use has been made of such information; and it is more recently that statistics have been brought into close connection with political economy. There were 'bills of mortality' in

[1] Petty also wrote on general economic subjects.
[2] See the article on *Statistics* in the *Encyclopædia Britannica* (ninth edition).

England in the reign of Henry VIII.; but the first census was taken in 1801, and did not extend to Ireland, while the project of taking it all was met by stubborn superstitious objections. Adam Smith had "no great faith in political arithmetic"; and the most trustworthy geographers of the last century were considered to be those who did not attempt to estimate the population of their own European countries. Malthus seems to have been almost the first professed economist of real eminence, who made any extensive use of statistics; and he states that the "science may be said yet to be in its infancy."

The scientific treatment, then, of figures is comparatively modern; but they are full of pitfalls for the unscientific. "Statistics," Mr. Giffen writes, "are almost always difficult," and "no" statistical "table almost can be used without qualification and discretion." "Figures themselves," Mr. Göschen remarks, "never lie, but every one must admit that there is no sound and accurate material which can be so easily handled for the special purpose of the compiler as statistics can." It is, then, in the handling of figures that mistakes and abuses arise; and they may occur either in the collection of the figures, or in their arrangement and interpretation.

The sources of information may be misleading and inadequate, and it may be impossible to draw any certain conclusions from the figures which have been collected. The sources may, indeed, be so many in number that the error proceeding from one is neutralised by that proceeding from another; or, if the method of collection in different cases be uniform, the resulting error in each case may be uniform also, and neglected for the purposes of comparison. But these methods of eliminating error are not always

possible, and the evidence of figures is often tainted by
a vicious or defective mode of collection.

Nor does the liability to error end at this stage; for the
arrangement and interpretation of figures, which have been
industriously and intelligently collected, require a high degree
of judicial and vigilant discrimination. It is, for instance, a
common practice to compare the growth in the trade of different countries by a standard of *percentages*. But this method
of measurement, as Mr. Giffen has shown, may mislead, in
consequence of the different amounts on which the *percentages* are reckoned. "The increase from zero, or all but
zero, to an appreciable amount of trade, makes an enormous
change in the ' percentages'; and the only safe plan is to
state the original amounts on which the *percentages* have been
reckoned as well as the *percentages* themselves. Nor, again,
is it so easy a task as it may appear to strike an *average*
correctly,[1] and more than one different method, yielding
different results, may be employed.

The execution of statistical work of real value is thus a
matter of difficulty; and the requisite qualities are by
no means the natural inheritance of all men. The ability
and success of Jevons were due to some remarkable gifts,
which were strengthened by education and training.

He was born at Liverpool in 1835; and, as a boy, he
was said to be "thoughtful" and "eager to acquire information." He declared himself that he "often felt a positive
pain in passing any object which" he "could not understand the construction and meaning of." He had, then, that
first qualification for statistical work, which consists in a
habit of keen and pertinacious observation. And this habit
was strengthened by his very deficiences. His shyness

---

[1] See below, pp. 172-4.

and reserve rendered him somewhat solitary in his play in childhood, and was shown by his fondness for long walks by himself during his life in London at University College School in 1850 and 1851, and afterwards as a student of the College from 1851 to 1854. It exhibited itself during the years as assayer of the Mint in Sydney, which followed from 1854 to 1859, in his abstention from society, and during his later life as Lecturer and then Professor at Owens College, Manchester from 1863 to 1876, and afterwards at University College, London from 1876 to 1880, in the difficulty he seems to have experienced in expressing himself at first in speech or writing. It may have led him at times into unhealthy self-examination; but it undoubtedly encouraged his habits of reflection, and observation of fact, and threw him back on his own un-aided powers and resources.

Again, his early intellectual training familiarised him with the theoretical methods of scientific investigation; and his 'favourite study' during his first period at University College, London was 'physical science.' At the age of eighteen he was offered the post of assayer at the Mint in Sydney with an annual salary of some seven hundred pounds; and, although he accepted the offer with reluctance, and the full intention, from which he never swerved, to return as soon as he could to England, the post must have afforded him leisure for independent study, which he might not otherwise have been able to pursue, and accustomed him to habits of precise investigation and measurement. It was after he had passed through this preliminary training that, on his return to England, and the resumption, at the age of twenty-four, of his studies at University College, he felt attracted to mental and moral philosophy. He had already acquired, as he said himself, a "capacity of seeing the sameness and the difference of things"; and, although he was conscious of possessing little power of memory, and less of imagination, he believed that he could "seize" upon "one or two" thoughts, and "develop them into something symmetrical." This faculty had its dangers; and, in his statistical work, it occasioned one notion at least which has been considered fanciful,[1] just as in that part of his writings which was more generally economic it led him perhaps to form an exaggerated estimate of the influence of utility in the determination of value.[2] It also resulted in a treatment of almost every subject, or branch of a subject, which he took up, which was so original in conception, and independent in execution, that it tended to create an impression of a wider divergence than seems to have really existed between his work and that of preceding writers. But the faculty was unquestionably of great value in the performance of statistical work, and it was eminently calculated to incline the possessor towards statistical study.

It was, then, little wonder that almost his first literary project of any magnitude was a *Statistical Atlas*, and that the pamphlet, which he wrote in 1863 on a *Serious Fall in the Value of Gold*, attracted the complimentary notice of some of the older living economists. His book on the *Coal Question*, which was published in 1865, with the object of drawing attention to the "probable exhaustion of our coal mines," was based on statistical data, and confessedly influenced Mr. Gladstone, who was then Chancellor of the Exchequer, in making provision for the more speedy reduction of the National Debt. His little treatise on *Money and the Mechanism of Exchange*, published ten years later, contains statistical facts as well as an exposition of

[1] See below, p. 171.　　　[2] See above, p. 108.

monetary theory; and his sudden death in 1882, while
bathing at Bexhill, left behind an impression that it was not
only a logician and economist, but also, in a very special
degree, a statistician, who had been removed in the prime of
his intellectual powers at the early age of forty-six. He
possessed a large measure of the two qualities which, it
seems, should be combined in the person of the successful statistician; for he united great theoretical ability
with keen observation of salient fact.

His statistical studies have been collected together under
the title of *Investigations in Currency and Finance.* He had
formed the collection himself; but it was not published
until after his death. The papers, of which it consists, "fall
into two groups," one of which deals with the periodic
fluctuations of prices, and the other with currency questions.
In the latter group are included discussions on "bi-metallism,"
and "an ideally perfect system of currency," together with the
results of a statistical inquiry into the "condition of the gold
coinage of the United Kingdom." But it is perhaps in the
former group that his statistical ability is more conspicuous;
and the different papers, although written at different times,
furnish the successive stages of a connected inquiry.

The value of such an inquiry as that which is here conducted
into the fluctuations of prices is very considerable. The
elaborate researches made by PROFESSOR THOROLD ROGERS
into the *History of Agriculture and Prices in England* illustrate the importance of records of prices as evidence of the
economic conditions of the past; and it is sometimes said
that the greatest economic evil of the present is irregularity
of employment. That irregularity is connected with changes
in prices, whether they are due to speculation, or to 'freaks'
of fashion demanding one kind of goods, and ceasing to
demand another, or to miscalculations of the future; and

the establishment of 'greater industrial stability,' is, as Professor Foxwell has said,[1] a question of diminishing " price fluctuations." But the first step towards providing a remedy is to diagnose the disease ; and such statistical investigations as that of Jevons into the periodic fluctuations of prices are one means of discovering their nature and causes.

. In this investigation he made considerable and effective use of what is known as the 'graphic method' of statistics. It consists in invoking the aid of the eye to assist the brain, by representing numbers, and the relations between them, by means of graphic processes. A French statistician [2] has pithily said that such a method is to figures what in a drama the action is to the story. The method may take several forms. A recent American writer [3] has used lines of different length to represent numbers of different magnitude. The eye is able to grasp the differences and the similarities in a number of lines with greater rapidity and ease than the brain can display in dealing with a number of figures ; and the lines may remain imprinted on the memory when the figures have passed away. Another variety of the method is to construct a diagram, say, of rectangular shape, to represent the population of the British colonies, and to break this up into smaller rectangles representing the population of the colonies of other nations, and other rectangles representing the population of those nations, and of the United Kingdom. The eye can take in the meaning of the diagram almost at a glance ; and it can interpret

[1] In a lecture on *Irregularity of Employment and Fluctuations in Prices* contained in *The Claims of Labour*.

[2] M. Levasseur in a paper in the *Jubilee Volume of the Royal Statistical Society*.

[3] Mr. Edward Atkinson in his *Industrial Progress of the Nation*.

with similar rapidity the significance of a map, which is differently coloured, or shaded, to represent different degrees of density of population.

The line, the diagram, and the shaded or coloured map, are thus varieties of the graphic method; and, although it is easily liable to misuse, and should be employed with discretion, it undoubtedly conduces to the easier and more effectual understanding of figures.   But the special variety which Jevons employed was that of the curve.   A curve is drawn to exhibit the fluctuations in price of a certain commodity during a certain period of time.   Two lines are drawn at right angles to one another, one in a horizontal and one in a perpendicular direction.   The horizontal line is divided into different spaces indicating days, or weeks, or months, or years; and the perpendicular line is similarly divided into spaces showing the pence, or shillings, or pounds, or tens or hundreds or thousands of pounds, for which a certain quantity of the commodity sells.   The curve of price starts from the point in the perpendicular line which indicates the price at which it is selling at the beginning of the period under consideration.   At the end of one of the divisions of that period the price may have altered; and, if it has done so, two lines are drawn at right angles respectively to the perpendicular and the horizontal line, starting from the point in the former which marks the present price, and from that in the latter which indicates the end of the old and beginning of the new division of the period of time.   These lines intersect one another, and the curve is continued until it cuts the point of intersection.   And so it inclines upwards or downwards as the price rises or falls, and the eye is enabled to comprehend at a glance the meaning of several figures.

The method of curves has further advantages.   Several

curves may be drawn representing respectively the prices of
different articles; and examination may disclose similarities
in the inclinations of the different curves, which point to the
probability of the same, or a similar, cause, affecting the
prices of the different articles. Or, again, though one part
of a single curve may be higher or lower than another,
careful observation may detect a similarity between the
changes at the higher and those at the lower level; and this
similarity may indicate the operation of the same, or a
similar, cause on different occasions. It was his power of
detecting these similarities which enabled Jevons to employ
so effectively the method of curves; and he believed himself
that he possessed a " capacity of seeing the sameness and
the difference of things.

He conducted an examination into the published weekly
accounts of the Bank of England, of which a complete
series existed since the passing of the Bank Charter Act in
1844. He drew statistical curves showing the variations in
the circulation of bank-notes, and in the amounts of bullion,
and of private, and public deposits, and securities, in different
weeks. He discovered a *monthly* variation, which occurred
about every fourth day of the month, and was due to the
fact that bills were generally settled on that day. There
was also a *quarterly* variation, which was due to the payment
of the dividends on the National Debt, and the "general
custom of settling rents and other accounts at the quarter-
days." And there was a curious further variation which
recurred with regularity in the autumn. There was what
he called an "*autumnal pressure in the money market*," when
the harvest was being gathered in, and large money-pay-
ments were due. The rate of discount, or the terms on
which money could be borrowed, rose; for money was

urgently needed.   The rate of bankruptcy increased; for more people failed to meet their monetary engagements. The prices of wheat and of consols fell; for the harvest was being gathered in, and investment was less desirable than cash in hand.

There is, in short, as the *Economist* stated, a "sort of *tide* in the cash transactions of the country which periodically empties and fills the Bank till.   At the close of every quarter there is a strong outgoing current"; for the "non-banking classes" "get their money." Salaries, wages, and small dividends are paid.   But, besides this *quarterly* variation, there is, as Jevons showed, an *annual* autumnal drain, which renders October and November the most critical period of the year regarded from a monetary stand-point.   In agricultural industry and other out-door employments, in pleasure-seeking and in travelling, a great amount of money is "dispersed" in wages and other payments throughout the summer months; and many of the recipients have no banking accounts, and keep the money by them in hard cash.   The country banks are the first to feel the drain which is thus occasioned, and they pass it on to their London agents, and, through them, to the head of the banking hierarchy, the Bank of England.

Bringing next under consideration the prices of ordinary commodities Jevons detected a variation which recurred at longer intervals.   Every ten years or so a *commercial crisis*[1] seemed to take place.   There had been one in 1825, another in 1836, another in 1847, and another in 1857, and yet another in 1866.   At such a time prices rapidly declined from the point which they had reached in a previous period of commercial activity, and every one was eager to obtain cash, and distrustful of credit.   The state of trade, to quote

---

[1] See above, pp. 149—154.

the words of Lord Overstone, "revolves apparently in an established cycle. First we find it in a state of quiescence, —next, improvement,—growing confidence,—prosperity,— excitement,—over-trading,—convulsion,—pressure,—stagnation,—distrust,—ending again in quiescence."

Jevons saw that this cycle seemed to occupy with remarkable uniformity periods of about ten years in duration; and he noticed that the beginning of speculative activity and growing prosperity often appeared to coincide with favourable harvests. If, then, the weather, on which the "success of the harvest" certainly depended, could be brought into any causal connection with the "solar period"—with that "periodic variation of the sun's condition which was first discovered in the alternate increase and decrease of area of the" so-called "sun-spots," and was "also marked by the occurrence" of storms and "other meteorological disturbances"—it did not seem entirely fanciful to suppose that the ebb and flow of the tide of commerce had some connection with the alterations in the spots on the sun. Nor was there much doubt that the rainfall was "more or less influenced" by the "changes in the sun's condition."

This theory has been subjected to severe criticism, and sometimes to ridicule; and the evidence advanced to support it is far from conclusive. But, whatever be or be not its real value, and whatever be the amount of error involved in supposing that the cycle of trade is decennial, and not longer or shorter, there is no question of the existence of an ebb and flow in the tide of trade, and there is no doubt that these fluctuations recur with some regularity, and that the influences, which produce the one, have a tendency to set in operation influences, which in their turn produce the other. A curve of prices would indicate such fluctuations, by its movements upwards and downwards, over and above the movements occasioned by those fluctuations, which occurred at more frequent intervals, and lasted for a shorter period of time, or were due to special causes affecting particular commodities.

The last periodic fluctuation in prices, which Jevons noticed, extended over a yet longer period. Besides the smaller variations in the curve, it might take a general sweep upwards or downwards, according as the value of gold fell or rose, and the precious metal became more or less abundant compared with the work of exchanging which it performed. The direction given to the curve by this influence was, like that occasioned by alternating periods of commercial prosperity and depression, ascertained by means of an average of prices; and the method of obtaining this average which Jevons followed was one variety of what is known as the method of *index numbers*.

A certain number of articles of ordinary consumption are selected; and the average wholesale price for a period of time and a district of country, or, it may be, the selling price prevailing in a particular representative market on a certain representative day, is ascertained in the case of each separate article. The average price prevailing at the time from which the investigator starts, is regarded as equivalent to 100, and, therefore, the price of all the articles selected,—say, twenty-two in number,—is equivalent to 2,200. He then ascertains in each succeeding period of time, in the same way as he did in the first, the average price for each of the twenty-two articles, and discovers how large is the percentage of advance or decline which their new prices exhibit when compared with the old. He adds these percentages to the original 100, or deducts them, as the case may be, and then adds together the numbers separately obtained for each of the twenty-two articles into one grand total, and, measuring the rise or fall of general prices by the extent to which this number exceeds or falls short of the original 2,200, draws his curve accordingly.

This method of selecting twenty-two articles, and comparing their prices, has been adopted for a series of years by the *Economist* newspaper.[1] But it has been contended on various grounds that the average obtained is unreliable. Some critics have urged that the articles, which are selected, are not representative of general consumption. They consist largely of raw materials, and it is a well-known fact of economic experience that the cost of transforming raw materials into manufactured commodities tends to decrease relatively to the cost of procuring the raw materials themselves, as civilisation advances. If, then, the *index number* obtained from the prices of the twenty-two articles exhibits a fall, the fall might be greater if the prices of manufactured commodities had been included ; and, as they are concerned in a larger number of transactions, their omission is misleading, and the resulting average is an inadequate representation of the changes in the purchasing-power of money.

Again, it is argued by some critics that the *index number* of the *Economist* does not include a sufficient number of articles to make it certain that the result is not unduly affected by circumstances which are peculiar to some one or two. The more articles are included, the more likely it is that some special circumstance peculiar to one article, and acting in one direction, will be counteracted by another special circumstance peculiar to another article, and acting in the opposite direction. But the number of twenty-two is insufficient ; and cotton goods, which were affected by a

[1] This *index number* is due to WILLIAM NEWMARCH, who also edited and continued the *History of Prices* (1782—1857) commenced by THOMAS TOOKE.

special scarcity during the American Civil War, enter largely in some form or other into the articles selected.

Thirdly, and lastly, it has been said that the twenty-two articles are not all equally important.   Some are more, and others are less, generally consumed, and therefore some are more, and others less, frequently exchanged against money. To find, then, the changes in the average purchasing-power of money greater weight should be given to the former than to the latter.   This may be done in various ways; but, if it is not, the average is unreliable.

Jevons was aware of such objections as these when he wrote his pamphlet on a *Serious Fall in the Value of Gold*. He uses himself, by preference, a " geometric average "[1] of prices, instead of simply adding together the figures obtained for the separate articles; and he includes within the scope of his inquiries a larger number of articles.   His pamphlet, which is reprinted in his *Investigations in Currency and Finance*, is an endeavour to trace the effects of the discoveries of gold which were made some forty years ago in California and Australia.[2]   In consequence of these discoveries the curve of prices took an upward, while latterly it has seemed to take a downward direction.   This bend of the curve can be detected in a diagram covering a series of years.   It rises and falls, as the tide of commerce flows and ebbs; and it rises and falls, beyond these fluctuations, as the value of gold grows less or greater.   The lowest and the highest point of one tide of commerce are lower or higher than those of another, or, at any rate, the average level of the curve during one tide is lower or higher than during another, according as the value of gold is rising or falling, and prices are declining or advancing.

[1] " To take the geometric mean of two ratios we must multiply them together and extract the square root of the product."   [2] See p. 124.

These changes in the value, or purchasing power, of gold affect different classes of the community in different ways and degrees. Jevons pointed out that those who received 'fixed incomes,' and made 'fixed payments,' were unaffected; for, if the money was worth less when they received it, it was also worth less when they paid it away, and *vice versâ*. Nor were those persons affected whose receipts and payments both varied with the variations in the value of gold. But persons who received 'fixed incomes,' and had to make 'variable payments,' suffered by a rise and benefited by a fall in prices, and persons who received 'variable incomes,' and had to make 'fixed payments,' were situated in the reverse position. When the value of gold fell, and the prices of commodities rose, debtors benefited at the expense of creditors, for the money went further in the purchase of commodities at the time when they contracted the loan than it did when they had to repay it. In the opposite condition of affairs creditors benefited at the expense of debtors. The burden of national debt is lessened at a time of rising, and increased at a time of falling prices; and those engaged in trade, who have generally borrowed money, are rendered more cheerful by rising, and more despondent by falling prices. If they are manufacturers, they may have bought their raw material, and made their contract for wages, at a time when prices were at a higher, or lower, figure than that at which they stand when they sell their manufactured commodities. In the former case they lose, and, in the latter they gain. It is, then, little wonder that they make their voices heard in rejoicing or complaint, while the wage-earning classes, whose wages do not rise or fall as fast as prices, are generally, for the time at least, gainers when prices fall, and losers when they rise.

With the treatment of this great fluctuation Jevons' inquiries reach their final stage. Their value as contributions to the development of speculative theory is evident, but they are scarcely less valuable in their relation to practical affairs. Before any approach can be made towards that greater steadiness of prices, which on many grounds appears desirable, a knowledge of the nature and causes of their fluctuations must be acquired. But, if the true meaning of the past can be interpreted correctly, the prediction of the future becomes less impossible; and prevision may mean precaution. The knowledge that the autumn is the critical season of the financial year, and that there is, in the nature of things, likely to be a drain on the cash-reserve of the Bank of England at that time, is calculated to lead the directors to make provision for anticipating the drain, and replenishing their reserve. The knowledge that there is an ebb and flow in the tide of commerce may lead men to see danger ahead, to interpret the signs of the times, to observe and understand the commercial weather-glass, to avert, or protect themselves against, the coming storm. The knowledge that the curve of general prices falls or rises as the value of gold rises or falls may lead to the study, and possibly to the improvement, of monetary systems in order to diminish price-fluctuations, and to such an adjustment of long bargains to these changes as to avoid apparent, or real, injustice. Such statistical investigations as those made by Jevons furnish the means of gaining part of that knowledge, which in these cases unquestionably is power, if only it is not of such a character as to justify the application of another proverb, which lays stress on the dangerous nature of inadequate knowledge.

CHAPTER VIII.

HENRY FAWCETT. 1833—1884.
ARNOLD TOYNBEE. 1852—1883.

SOCIAL REFORM.

Political Economy and Social Reform—Fawcett as a Theoretical Economist—His Practical Qualities—His Courage and Independence —His Blindness—His Criticism of Indian Finance—His Common Sense—His Generous Sympathy—His Individualistic Attitude towards Social Reform.

Toynbee's Life—His Writings—His Personal Influence—The Practical Aims of his Theoretical Study—The Relations between Economic Theory and Practical Social Reform—Cairnes' Argument—Its Value —Its Defects—The Historical Method—Toynbee's Review of the Older Economists—The Wages-fund Theory—Newer Theories of Wages—The Limitations of 'Natural Liberty'—Education—Factory Legislation—The 'Gulf' in the Theory of *Laissez-faire*—Toynbee's Moderation—His Approval of Theory—His 'Radical Socialism.'

POLITICAL economy has been sometimes represented as condemning uniformly all schemes of social reform, and supporting the rich and powerful classes, who are prone to be content with the existing order, in their opposition to the poor, who fondly imagine that any change cannot fail to improve their own condition. Such a conception is indorsed by popular opinion. It is found on the pages of novels like Mr. Besant's *Children of Gibeon*, it formed the theme of the passionate denunciations of Carlyle, and

N

it furnishes the grounds for the distrust, which prompts the feeling that, "if Political Economy is against the working man, it behoves the working-man to be against Political Economy."

And yet, on a broad view of the history which we have been examining, such a conception appears erroneous; for most of the English economists have felt and expressed a wish to improve the condition of society, and their sympathies have generally inclined to the side of the poorer and weaker members. They have, indeed, been anxious to effect a real and not an imaginary improvement, and to attack the disease of poverty at its roots rather than procure a temporary mitigation of its outward symptoms; but, although their heads may have been hard, their hearts have usually been tender. Adam Smith may have committed an error in thinking that there was a "Scotchman inside every man;"[1] but the direction of his sympathies was unmistakable, and he was very eager to secure for the workman the free disposal of his "most sacred and inviolable property" in the labour of his hands. Malthus was impatient with fanciful schemes of ideal societies, but his interest in the poor was real and practical. Even the abstract Ricardo was evidently anxious to improve the condition of the wage-earning classes. "The friends of humanity," he writes, "cannot but wish that in all countries the labouring classes should have a taste for comforts and enjoyments, and that they should be stimulated by all legal means in their exertions to procure them." Nor could the enthusiasm of Mill for the advancement of society be doubted, while Cairnes in his *Slave Power* exposed the misery caused by the institution of slavery,

[1] See above, p. 10.

and in his *Leading Principles* was manifestly oppressed by the fear of a deterioration in the condition of the labourer. The *Methods of Social Reform* of Jevons are a proof of his interest in the promotion of social reform.

But the two economists, whose work we are now about to notice, supply perhaps the most convincing refutation of the popular idea of political economy as a 'dismal science' opposed to social reform. They were both social reformers, although they approached the matter from different stand-points; and they both brought their theoretical principles to bear on their practical action.

We have already seen how one English economist displayed remarkable fortitude in the endurance of physical pain.[1] But the courageous resolution of Cairnes was paralleled by that of HENRY FAWCETT. Immediately after his death, in 1884, Mr. Gladstone wrote to his father that[2] "there had been no public man of our day whose remarkable qualities had been more fully recognised by his fellow-countrymen and more deeply imbedded in their memories."

It would be incorrect to say that he made any considerable contribution to the development of economic theory.[3] His *Manual of Political Economy* was for the most part, as it was intended to be, a summary of Mill's larger work. His book on *Free Trade and Protection*, which was published in 1878, expounded the authorised principles of the subject, so far as it was theoretical. But his strength seems to have lain rather in the domain of practice. Those chapters of his *Manual*, in which he dealt with the practical facts of the Poor Law, or of Co-operation, were the more

[1] See above, p. 119.
[2] Cf. Leslie Stephen's *Life of Henry Fawcett*, p. 465.
[3] See above, p. 117.

original; and his work as administrator of the Post Office, and as critic of Indian finance, was marked by practical qualities of a high order. He kept, in fact, always before him the practical aims of theoretical inquiry, and he consistently conformed his practice to his theory.

The feature of his character, which made perhaps the most indelible impression on the public mind, was his indomitable courage and independence. At a most promising period of life, when he had completed his academic career at Cambridge by attaining high mathematical honours, and winning a Fellowship at Trinity Hall, he suddenly met with a grave physical calamity. At the age of twenty-five he was deprived of his eyesight by an accidental shot from his father's gun. "It was a blow to a man," he said, addressing a meeting at Brighton in after years, "but in ten minutes he had made up his mind to face his difficulty bravely," and to adhere to his old pursuits as far as possible. And face it accordingly he did. His first words on reaching home were purposely intended to cheer his relations; and visitors to the house during the following days remarked that his father seemed more distressed than himself. He did not abandon his rowing, riding, skating, or fishing. Nor did he swerve from that intention to enter Parliament, to which he had given expression when a boy at school. He fulfilled this intention; and he rose to be Postmaster-General in Mr. Gladstone's administration of 1880. So much, indeed, did he accomplish that his infirmity was almost forgotten, and he "claimed tacitly to have no allowance made" for it.

This courageous independence was shown in his attitude on political questions, and it coloured his economic thought. It intensified that fear and abhorrence of the degrading effects of pauperism, and that admiration for the independent spirit and self-reliant efficacy of co-operation, to which he gave expression in two little books on the *Economic Position of the British Labourer* in 1865, and on *Pauperism: its Causes and its Remedies* in 1871. It also characterised his action in Parliament in connection with *Indian Finance*, on which, in 1880, he published some articles. He offered a stubborn resistance to all the official attempts which were made to stifle his inquiries, and he compelled the thorough investigation of his arguments before Parliamentary Committees. He insisted that India was essentially a poor country, and that extreme caution and fairness were needed in the management of its finances, because its sources of revenue were 'inelastic,' and its expenditure was elastic and increasing. The revenue derived from the land-tax, which was fixed for long periods in some districts, and in others in perpetuity, did not admit of substantial increase. The revenue derived from opium was precarious, and that derived from salt was a tax on a prime necessity of Indian life, while the proceeds arising from the other sources of customs, excise, and stamps, were inconsiderable. But the expenditure on the other hand was elastic. The 'military expenditure' and the 'cost of administration' were continually growing, the loss occasioned by the 'fall in the exchange' of silver for gold was increasing, and the Indian Government had to make larger remittances to England in payment of debt, while the interest due on account of such public improvements as railways and works of irrigation, which the Government undertook or assisted, was becoming greater. There was consequently no surplus to meet such recurring emergencies as those occasioned by famine.

Fawcett's criticism of Indian finance disclosed a second quality of his nature; and that was the possession of shrewd common sense.   After his accident he deliberately set himself to learn to smoke, and to improve his taste for music, because such occupations would help him to pass the time independently of the attention of others.   In his administration of the Post Office he was ready to consider and adopt improvements, however unimportant they might seem, if they only tended to the greater convenience of the public. And, similarly, in Indian affairs he addressed himself from the outset to finance alone, with which his economic knowledge and training qualified him to deal.   Above all things he endeavoured to secure the correct keeping of accounts, and he insisted on the paramount importance of good finance to the interests of the Indian people.   Throughout his life he always proceeded on a few broad simple principles; and, while this habit rendered him a clear and forcible expositor, both in his writings, and in his lectures as Cambridge Professor of Political Economy from 1863 to his death in 1884, it sometimes tended to make him neglect difficulties, or omit qualifications.   But it was an advantage rather than a drawback in connection with Indian finance; for it was only broad simple principles which could be made intelligible and interesting to the English people.

A third characteristic of Fawcett's nature was his generous sympathy for the oppressed, and his abhorrence of mean or dishonourable conduct.   He endeavoured to secure the preservation of commons in England on behalf of the agricultural labourer.   He tried to encourage the thrift of the poor by affording, through the medium of the Post Office, increased facilities for saving.   He defended the interests of the unrepresented Indian peoples in Parliament, and earned

the title of ' Member for India.' He required an account of
the partnership which existed between England and India;
and, although he may have been sometimes accused of
exaggeration, his advocacy was inspired by generosity, and
directed by common sense, and he succeeded in effecting
a change in the general tone and temper with which Indian
affairs were treated and discussed.

While he was thus led by his generous sympathies to give
practical effect to his economic theories, his independence
of character combined with his appreciation of plain broad
principles to produce a profound distrust of the interference
of the State with individual liberty. He opposed any
scheme which might, by substituting collective for individual
action, tend ultimately to weaken the independence and
self-reliance of individuals; and he relied for the improvement of society mainly on the stimulus of individual interest
and intelligence. He was not indeed averse to the action
of the State, if, as in the case of the Post Office, it was
directed to assist the thrift of the poor, and to elicit self-
help; but he had a wholesome dislike, which he did not
conceal, for gigantic schemes of improvement, which, proceeding by the easy method, as it appeared, of using the
resources and machinery of the State, discouraged the
voluntary and independent experiments of private individuals,
and perhaps imposed an increasing burden of taxation on
those who were just struggling to keep themselves from
pauperism. / His social reform was strongly individualistic./

ARNOLD TOYNBEE inclined in the opposite direction.
His life was very brief; but his influence has survived him.
From his father, who formed many projects of improvement,
he seems to have imbibed an early tendency towards social

reform.   He felt himself an attraction for the army; and it
is not altogether fanciful to ascribe to this inclination the
abhorrence, amounting to pugnacity, which he seems to
have entertained for social injustice and oppression.   For
two years he resided at a military college; but then, thinking
his choice mistaken, he abandoned it.   Eighteen years of
age found him passing a year in solitary study of the philosophy of history in a retired Dorsetshire village; and in this
plan we may perhaps detect the genius and purpose of a
social reformer.   Two years afterwards he went to Oxford,
where he passed under the influence of the inspiring associations of that ancient and beautiful seat of learning,
which were especially calculated to awaken a response in
his sympathetic imaginative nature.   He began to exercise
the magnetic influence, which was perhaps his most conspicuous gift; and, in the congenial companionship of
intellectual friends, he formed noble ideals and aspirations.
"As to position in life," he wrote, "the position I wish to
attain is that of a man consumed with the thirst after
righteousness."   He was prevented by the ill-health, which
dogged his career, from reading for honours; but, not long
after taking his degree, he was appointed tutor to the
probationers for the Civil Service of India then residing at
Balliol College.

He devoted himself especially to the study of political
economy; and he kept continually before his mind the
responsibility involved in the training of future administrators
of Indian government.   It was partly at least for this
reason that he sought, with aid of the 'historical method'
of inquiry, to show the circumstances amongst which the
doctrines of the older economists had originated, and to
emphasise the relative nature of their application to other

countries and times. But his economic studies were also directed and stimulated by the eagerness with which he looked forward to social reform in England itself. He spent some time in lodgings in Whitechapel, to render himself acquainted with the conditions and feelings of the poor; and, discovering that he had a capacity for speech, he delivered popular addresses on economic topics to audiences of working-men and employers in Bradford and other manufacturing towns. The strain of these extemporaneous addresses combined with the multiplicity of his other interests and labours to exhaust a constitution which was always frail; and, after two lectures in London in 1883 on Mr. George's *Progress and Poverty*, he was attacked by an illness, of which he died within seven weeks.

He was only thirty years old, and this consideration must affect any judgment that is passed on his writings. They have not had, in most cases, the benefit of his personal revision, although they have been edited with loving and attentive care. They are fragmentary, and contain apparent inconsistencies, which more mature thinking might have removed. But they form some of the most attractive pieces of economic literature; and they are full of an inspiring, yet reasoned, enthusiasm. They consist of an essay on *Ricardo and the Old Political Economy*, some lectures, which give the title to the book in which his writings are collected, on the *Industrial Revolution in England* of the eighteenth century, and three popular addresses on the subjects of *Wages and Natural Law*, *Industry and Democracy*, and *Are Radicals Socialists?* together with some minor fragments.

But his personality exercised an influence of which his writings afford an inadequate idea. The Master of Balliol

has remarked[1] that the "really interesting and striking
thing in his life was not what he actually produced, but
Himself, that is to say, his simplicity and disinterestedness,
his sweet and lovely example, his unlikeness to anybody
else." Professor Marshall has described[2] him as the "ideal
modern representative of the mediæval saint; strong every
way, but with all other parts of his nature merged and
contained in an earnest and tender love towards God and
man." It is in part at least to his memory that those university and school 'settlements' are due, which have been
established of recent years in the poorer districts of some
of our great cities, to promote sympathy and intercourse
between the members of different classes, and to extend
the influence and advantages of intellectual culture. At
any rate it has been thought that to no name could the first
of those settlements be more fittingly linked than that of
Toynbee.[3] He was essentially a social reformer, to whom
the practical improvement of society was the end and
motive of all his theoretical study.

This relation between economic theory and practice has
been sometimes misconceived; and, to avoid this misconception, Cairnes contended[4] that the appropriate attitude
of political economy in the matter of social reform was
that of neutrality. He maintained that political economy
was "a science in the same sense in which Astronomy,
Dynamics, Chemistry, Physiology are sciences." The
"object" of the "recognised physical sciences" is "not

[1] In a memoir prefixed to the *Industrial Revolution*, p. xviii.
[2] In a preface to the present writer's *Industrial Peace*, p. viii.
[3] *I.e.* Toynbee Hall, in Whitechapel.
[4] In an essay on "Political Economy and Laissez-faire," in *Essays in Political Economy: Theoretical and Applied*, pp. 252, etc.

to attain tangible results, not to prove any definite
thesis, not to advocate any practical plan, but simply to
give light, to reveal laws of nature, to tell us what
phenomena are found together, what effects follow from
what causes." In the same way political economy "expounds" the "laws" of "wealth." It "stands apart from
all particular systems of social or industrial existence,"
"and is moreover absolutely neutral as between all." It
contributes "data towards the formation of a sound
opinion"; but, while these data may "go far to determine
our judgment," "they do not necessarily, and should not
in practice always do so. For there are few practical
problems which do not present other aspects than the
purely economical — political, moral, educational, artistic
aspects—and these may involve consequences so weighty as
to turn the scale against purely economic solutions. On
the relative importance of such conflicting considerations,
Political Economy offers no opinion, pronounces no judgment," thus "standing neutral between competing social
schemes," "as the science of Mechanics stands neutral
between competing plans of railway construction, in which
expense, for instance, as well as mechanical efficiency, is
to be considered." "It supplies the means, or, more
correctly, a portion of the means for estimating all; it
refuses to identify itself with any." "It has nothing to do
with *laissez-faire* any more than with communism; with
freedom of contract any more than with paternal government, or with systems of *status*." "It has no more
connection with our present industrial system than the
science of mechanics has with our present system of
railways. Our existing railway lines have been laid down
according to the best extant mechanical knowledge; but we

do not think it necessary on this account, as a preliminary to improving our railways, to denounce mechanical science." And yet " some social reformers, whose ideal of industrial life involves a modification of our existing system, have thought themselves called upon to denounce and deride economic science, as forsooth seeking to stereotype the existing forms of industrial life, and of course therefore opposed to their views." " But this is a complete mistake."

This argument, which is perhaps more clearly and forcibly stated by Cairnes than any other writer, is, as Toynbee recognised, important and suggestive. It lays a needed stress on considerations which are often forgotten or neglected.   It shows that the 'laws' of political economy are theoretical statements of the relations between certain facts, and not practical precepts enjoined in the imperative mood.   If the facts on which the laws are based undergo change, the condition of the laws continuing to be valid is that they should be submitted to a corresponding alteration ; and, with the lapse of time and progress of knowledge, the experience of facts, on which many economic 'laws' are grounded, may be extended and changed, as man himself is not a 'constant' invariable phenomenon.   The argument also establishes a distinction between the science of economics and the art of statesmanship or philanthropy, which is instructive in showing that other but purely economic considerations may enter into the determination of a practical problem.   But it is open to the danger of pushing the distinction between theory and practice too far, and of under-rating the influence exercised by our speculative opinions on our practical action.   "The maintenance of this neutrality is " Toynbee remarks, "practically impossible."

Hence probably it is that he insists on the importance of forming our theories as carefully, and testing their conclusions as constantly, as the nature of the case may admit. There is, he thinks, "no real opposition" between the Deductive and the Historical Method of inquiry.[1] "The apparent opposition is "due to a wrong use of deduction : to a neglect on the part of those employing it to examine closely their assumptions and to bring their conclusions to the test of fact." The Historical Method supplies the needful corrective. It "examines the actual causes of economic development and considers the influence of institutions, such as the mediæval guilds, our present land laws, or the political constitution of any given country, in determining the distribution of wealth." "And not only does it investigate the stages of economic development in a given country, but it compares them with those which have obtained in other countries and times." It is of "value because it makes us see where economic laws and precepts are relative." "Abstract propositions are seen in a new light when studied in relation to the facts which were before the writer at the time when he formulated them. So regarded they are at once more vivid and less likely to mislead."

In this spirit Toynbee reviews the teaching of the older economists. He traces the course of the "Industrial Revolution," which was effected in England at the close of the last and the opening of the present century. He shows how Adam Smith,[2] living on the eve of this revolution amid the relics of the routine and regulation of an older period, and imbued with a desire to restore the original simplicity and freedom of 'nature,' and a confidence in the power and disposition of God to cause the individual, freely seeking

---

[1] See above, chapter v.   [2] See chapter i.

his own interest, to promote, consciously or unconsciously, the common weal, advocated with passionate earnestness the removal of artificial barriers and the full establishment of "natural liberty." That seemed to be the paramount need of his time ; and he did not live to witness the distress, which accompanied free competition, in the early part of this century.

He was followed by Malthus,[1] who was not so thorough a supporter of "natural liberty." But at the time when he wrote the law of diminishing returns seemed to be applying to English agriculture with alarming reality, and population was continually increasing. The share, which the poorer classes could obtain of the wealth of the country, became less and less, and wages tended downwards to a bare subsistence. But, bad as was the condition of affairs in England, it was better than abroad ; and the explanation seemed to lie in the greater amount of her accumulated wealth, or capital. And so, putting two and two together, Malthus suggested—for he was, Toynbee maintains, the "founder" of the theory, though later economists may have been its immediate exponents—that wages were dependent upon the capital, which had been previously accumulated, and that the only methods of raising them were to increase the capital, or diminish the numbers of the population. This was the origin of the 'wages-fund' theory.

Malthus was contemporary with Ricardo,[2] who saw around him, when he wrote his *Principles of Political Economy and Taxation*, a busy, restless world, and based his theories on the universal prevalence of competition, according to which rent would rise, wages "remain about the same," and profits fall, as population increased.

[1] See chapter ii.   [2] See chapter iii.

All these economists were led by facts, which were especially prominent in their own time, to construct theories based upon this prominence; but other facts have since come into prominence, and the theories require alteration. The Ricardian theory of rent stands in need of qualification before it is applied to fact. Since the "wages-fund" theory was propounded, a fresh continent has been peopled in America, where, as President Walker has shown,[1] there was originally no accumulated store of capital, but there was a virgin soil, which yielded increasing rather than diminishing returns. No means existed of paying wages in advance, but ultimately higher wages could be given. And so the point of view was shifted. It was seen that, although wages might be advanced out of capital, the employer, whose functions as distinct from those of the capitalist have been brought into a prominence, which their separate importance deserves, by more recent economists,[2] would regard the prices which his goods were likely to fetch, and would offer wages accordingly. It was seen that an increase of population might be so far from trenching on the capital from which wages were paid, and diminishing the share of each labourer, that it might bring about an increase in that share by augmenting production by means of improved division and organisation of labour. It was seen that a similar result might follow from an increase in the efficiency of the labourer himself. He would not, indeed, be content, any more than in former times, to receive in the long run less than would enable him to live himself, and to bring up his children, according to the 'standard of comfort' to which he was accustomed. Nor would he in the long run receive more than left sufficient to give the capitalists, and the employers,

[1] In his book on the *Wages Question*.　[2] See above, p. 103.

the interest of capital, and the earnings of management, without which their co-operation would not be forthcoming. But both these limits were elastic; and within them wages might vary according as the sympathy of public opinion, the removal of legal restriction, the support of legal protection, or the resources of combination, might from time to time render the one or the other party the stronger. On these lines Toynbee showed how, led by the influence of facts, we have departed in our theories of wages from the comparatively inelastic conception of a 'wages-fund.'

Thirdly, and lastly, he pointed out that we may examine in a similar manner Adam Smith's advocacy of "natural liberty;" and it is here especially that the historical method has an important bearing on social reform. Later knowledge and inquiry seem to have shown the necessity, or at any rate the advantage, of some limitations of individual liberty. There are men, and at least there are women and children, engaged in industry, who suffer from disadvantages, which no economic forces seem of themselves likely to remove; and that free competition, which is suited to equal industrial competitors, may be fraught with mischief, when it prevails among those who are unequally situated. We must endeavour to secure for each individual the opportunity for full and free development; and this may imply legislative protection and assistance, as well as the removal of legislative restriction. We do not believe that men always know, and always seek, their true, permanent interests. They may be blinded by the passion of the moment, or they may be ignorant and weak. Nor do we think that the interests of the individual will always coincide with the interests of the community, for he may not reap the ultimate consequences of his action.

If, for example, we take the question of education, we may ask whether we can safely rely on the interest of parents in the education of their children. Can we be sure that, where parental affection is weak, the pecuniary advantages that may possibly result from the increased ability of the children to earn their living at an earlier age will be sufficiently real to the parents to make them incur certain and immediate expense? Can we be sure that, where they are ignorant and poor, they will be able to discern, and to satisfy, the interests of themselves or their children in a good education? Such considerations as these have suggested the advisability of national compulsory education; and they met with the approval of Fawcett as well as Toynbee. But, while Toynbee might have viewed with favour proposals for 'free education,' they would have aroused the distrust, and encountered the opposition, of Fawcett, as tending to weaken individual responsibility, and discourage voluntary effort.

Again, the influence of passion or prejudice, or the immediate concerns of the moment, may cause men to shut their eyes to the recognition of their true permanent interests. Honesty may be the 'best policy' in the long run; but we do not cease to hear of adulteration and jerry-building. The children, who were overworked in the factories during the early part of this century, might have proved more efficient workers in the end, had they received more humane and considerate treatment. But, apart from the fact that the masters, who showed the kindness, might not themselves have reaped the benefit, because the children might have gone to other factories, the pressing needs of the times, and of their own personal and immediate interests, led them, and the parents also, to neglect the permanent interests of

o

the children, and the nation as a whole. Such considerations have led to our elaborate code of Factory Laws; and, while Toynbee approved, Fawcett disliked and opposed, their extension to adult women, for fear that it would undermine individual independence.

But there is, as Toynbee saw, a "chasm to be bridged" in a theory of *laissez-faire* between the interests of the individual and those of the community, and between the existence and recognition of those interests. "This chasm," Cairnes declares, "has never been bridged. The advocates of the doctrine shut their eyes and leap over it." The interference of the State is sometimes needed to secure the permanent interests of the whole community, to incur present outlay for future benefit, and to help the weak and ignorant members to obtain the opportunity for that full development which, being for the ultimate benefit of all, might be sacrificed to the immediate interests of the few. This work of the State might, Toynbee held, be increased in the future; and he even went so far as to say: "The era of free trade and free contract is gone, and the era of administration has come."

This seems, however, to have been but a pardonable excess of emphasis; and he was by no means willing to pass to the extreme lengths of 'continental socialism.' "We shall have to carry out these measures," he remarks, "without undermining that old independence, the habit of voluntary association of which we are justly proud; for if we undermine that—that pride which has made the English workman sacrifice everything to keep himself out of the workhouse, which has made workmen bind themselves together in Friendly Societies, and Trades Unions, and Co-operative Societies, if we undermine that, then it would be better to leave our work undone." "Competition is neither good nor evil in itself. It is a force to be studied and controlled."

Nor, with all his eagerness for practical improvement, did he disdain theoretical inquiry. He could not, it is true, endure the hard, unemotional attitude, which some economists seemed to him to have adopted. They appeared to talk of matters involving suffering, if not death, to human beings, as if they were only specimens of the correctness of a theory. They seemed to regard the enactment of human dramas, concerned with the joys and the sorrows of men, from the stand-point of cool, critical spectators. If a man was thrown out of employment by a freak of fashion, they spoke glibly of the mobility of labour. If a woman or child was overworked in a factory, they complacently argued that such a course of action would in the end injure the employer, and he would not continue to pursue it. But Toynbee's nature was intensely sympathetic. He knew and felt that men, women, and children had passions and feelings, sympathies and antipathies, and that they could not with advantage be discussed like bales of wool, to be carried hither and thither, wherever they could earn a penny more.

But his sympathy was none the less tempered by sobriety. He recognised that without care, patience, and knowledge social reform might produce more mischief than benefit. He dwelt on the evils of a lax Poor Law with as much earnestness as Malthus himself. He condemned the extravagances of democratic revolutionary Socialists with as much vehemence as an economist of the straitest school. He exposed the fallacies of Mr. George in the last lectures which he delivered ; and in one of his popular addresses he analysed the different causes affecting the rate of wages with patient exhaustiveness. He wanted more rather than less economic study ; but it must be study which, without being soulless or passionless, took into consideration the varied interests of human life, and issued in practical action.   He inclined, it was true, in the direction of increased interference on the part of the State with individual liberty, and so far he was socialistic ; but his socialism might be more correctly described as the complement than the opposite of that individualism to which Fawcett inclined.

"The Radical creed, as I understand it," he remarks, " is this : We have not abandoned our old belief in liberty, justice, and self-help, but we say that under certain conditions the people cannot help themselves and that then they should be helped by the State representing directly the whole people.   In giving this State help we make three conditions : first, the matter must be one of primary social importance ; next, it must be proved to be practicable ; thirdly, the State interference must not diminish self-reliance." "We differ from Tory Socialism in so far as we are in favour, not of paternal, but of fraternal government, and we differ from Continental Socialism because we accept the principle of private property, and repudiate confiscation and violence." " To a reluctant admission of the necessity for State action, we join a burning belief in duty, and a deep spiritual idea of life."

INDEX.

*

www.ingramcontent.com/pod-product-compliance
Lightning Source LLC
Chambersburg PA
CBHW030820270326
41928CB00007B/825